PEN PAPER PRAYER

A TRUE STORY OF DEATH AND LIFE

BY

JAMES P. HOLMES

Edited by: Randy S. Rosenthal

MTS HARVARD DIVINITY SCHOOL

Proofread by: Frank W. Kresen

PROOF POSITIVE

Interior/Cover Design by: Kim Walsh

ARTISAN GRAPHIC DESIGN

jamespholmes.com

"This is a long way from life support"

ISBN 978-1-7344936-0-3

Coming This Fall

I bared my soul in writing PEN, PAPER, PRAYER, both the good and the bad. Re-living the whole experience was exhausting and difficult. As I say in my videos, "If I hadn't lived it, I wouldn't believe it." (jamespholmes.com)

I enjoy writing, telling a story. So, when PEN, PAPER, PRAYER was done I started writing for fun, as a release.

Out of this self-administered therapy, The Mailbox Mysteries, evolved. A series of books featuring Jack Harrington, whom, like myself, has suffered a traumatic brain injury. The book is fiction, but Jack's struggle is real.

The first volume, In My Fathers Foot Steps, Jack is un-officially recruited by the local Chief of police in Wellfleet, MA to look into his own father's death. The investigation has been "swept under the rug" by the State Police, further fanning the flames of suspicion that Jack's father, Walter Harrington, had been murdered, as most of the locals believed.

Walter was a good mail-man and an even better husband, father, and friend. His death was tragic enough, but murder in the sleepy sea-side town of Wellfleet?

Unfortunately, Walter would not be the last resident to die a suspicious death, leaving the town's residents on edge, and surrounded by a cloud of mystery.

Please visit jamespholmes.com for updated information about The Mailbox Mysteries release date.

Thanks,
Jim

PEN PAPER PRAYER
READER REVIEWS

Christopher R. Whiting

Independence, MO

Pen, Paper, Prayer, James Holmes story of dying and coming back to life, is a book overflowing with redemption and hope. I've read several books about NDE's (near death experiences) and none have explored, with such depth and honesty, what it must be like to lose your mortality, experience immeasurable bliss, and come back into your body. The author's struggles, following his taste of the unmitigated joy of the afterlife, resonated with me as I've often wondered how hard it would be to come back to this existence after experiencing heaven/nirvana. His ultimate redemption and renewed sense of purpose, after years of struggle, provide hope for all of us. For anyone who is wrestling with the meaning of their own mortality, or who is wondering what has happened to loved ones who have passed on, this is a must read. The book is well-written and hard to put down. I finished it in one sitting and highly recommend it.

Denise M. McShane

Stoughton, MA

Jim Holmes is a storyteller. He has crafted a tale that does what all good stories should do – elicit emotion in the reader. *Pen, Paper, Prayer* is compelling, informative, funny, heart-wrenching, and, most importantly, true! In this book, Jim bravely shares his innermost feelings regarding his struggles with his traumatic brain injury, long recovery, and desire to reclaim his life. He also lets us in on what happened to him when he died as a result of the car crash. He takes us on an amazing journey of survival and the incredible power of prayer. I am now far more aware of how a traumatic brain injury impacts not only the victim but also those who love that person as well. I am grateful to have read this book, for it has left me more spiritual. I am in awe of Jim's strength, honesty, courage, and the determination of the human spirit.

Kimberly A. Walsh
Kansas City, MO

5 stars! A Powerful and Compelling read!

I could not recommend a book more highly than I can this one. *Pen, Paper, Prayer,* is a true story that gives you **hope** for life after death. Jim's ability to communicate his experience during his time in heaven and his return to his body is simply amazing! As he shares his experience—you can *feel and see* his glimpse into eternity. It affirms the power of prayer and that miracles do happen. His miracle death and life experience also reveals how much we are loved by a presence unseen.

Jim's recount of his recovery and the love of his family makes this book especially hard to put down.

Jim's recovery is a true miracle, I recommend this book to everyone and *especially,* those who have or love someone with a brain injury.

CONTENTS

ABOUT THE AUTHOR

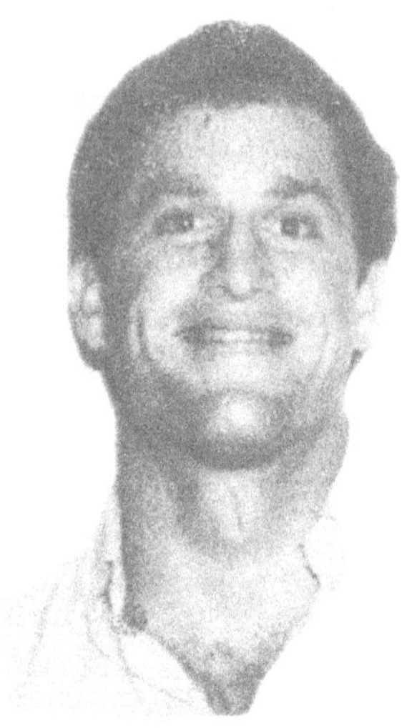

Driver's license photo 1979

"Courage is like love, it must have hope to nourish it."

Napoleon Bonaparte

I was born on February 10th, 1957 in Wareham, Ma. My parents, Phil and Jean Holmes, were living in Falmouth, Massachusetts, at the time. This is the town where I would be raised and attend public school. Graduating from Falmouth High school in 1975, I was pretty much done with formal education. Not really having a direction in life, I would attend and leave several colleges before settling down into a good job as an estimator and superintendent for a local construction company. After several years of excelling at and loving my job, I was in a terrible car accident. My life went completely off the rails, and I would never be the same. My death, new life, and unexpectedly strong relationship with God is what I have written about in *Pen, Paper, Prayer.*

I am a flawed person living a remarkable life. Remarkable in that, despite my shortcomings, and skeptical take on religion, I was given a second chance at life.

My tremendous injuries from a car accident killed me. Death was beautiful beyond words, and I was content to be dead.

Not only did I come back to life, but I would eventually flourish despite having lost part of my brain.

Recovering from my traumatic brain injury was a long and difficult process, one that I was forced to do on my own, never receiving one second of formal rehabilitation.

During this time, I struggled with; being alive again, relationships, drinking, self-worth, and an on-again, off-again relationship with God.

I just wasn't worthy of God's attention, or so I thought .

AUTHOR'S NOTE

This book is a work of narrative nonfiction. The characters are real, and the events depicted actually happened. Passages in which I narrate a person's thoughts and feelings are based on interviews with the subjects and witnesses. The characters are real, some of their names have been changed for privacy reasons. When I was twenty-three, I died of massive brain trauma and other injuries suffered in a car accident. Obviously, I have lived to tell about it. I recall dying, being dead, and coming back to life. That is when my thirty-six-year struggle began, as my brain healed, and I tried to adjust to being alive again.

For my 58th birthday, this past February (2015), my daughter, Molly, gave me the book *Proof of Heaven: A Neurosurgeon's Journey into the Afterlife,* written by Eben Alexander, who also had a near-death experience. I eagerly read the bestseller, seeking validation of my own death experience. About halfway through, I stopped reading. Though I connected with the beginning of his story (his description of dying), his experience of being dead was nothing like mine. Not that mine is "right," but what I experienced is almost beyond description, and it took me years to comprehend. I have since finished *Proof of Heaven,* just to make sure that I didn't sell his book short; my opinion has not changed.

I particularly wanted to read about his recovery—not so much physically, but how he handled the mental aspect of dying and then coming back to life. When I came back to this world, I was different. My spirit, which was released in death, had to go back to its less-prominent role in my being. My brain, which was damaged, had to integrate this new form of awareness into daily life. My awakened spirit, which is meant for existence in death, was now very prominent in me. This heightened spirit was now active in day-to-day life and very vulnerable to this physical world, where it was never meant to exist. The mixing of dominant forces to run my body, brain, and spirit, and the associated realities did not go so well. My recovery has been difficult and complex on so many levels that it has taken me thirty-six years to process and begin to understand what happened to me. I read Dr. Alexander's book because I needed to know that someone else had come back from being dead, had struggled to be normal again, and was at a loss for words to describe what they had witnessed, that their experience with God defied all words and logic.

The big question that haunted me continuously was *Why me? Not Why did I die?* but *Why was I allowed to live—to come back to life?* Many people have died from less damage to their bodies than what happened to me, or they survived and are severely handicapped. I know that I shouldn't question my tremendous good fortune. But still, *Why? Why save me—of all people?* I *can* understand God saving Eben Alexander's life, as he is a highly educated neurosurgeon saving patients and improving lives. Dr. Alexander, as I read, was happily married, raising a good family, and well respected in the medical field. I envision him as a "Norman Rockwell-ish" figure, a pillar of his community. But me? I have only a high school education, a job in construction, and I liked to drink beer and chase women. I was hardly worthy of God's attention—or so I thought. But I was saved despite my "nobody" status in life. There is no question that I survived against all odds. But I would more than merely *survive*—I would eventually *flourish*, despite my permanent injuries. The fact that God saw fit to save me—*me, of all people*—should encourage everyone, no matter who they are or what they've done, to live without fear of dying. I can tell you that dying is a beautiful experience and that death is nothing to be afraid of—neither your own nor the death of somebody you know.

So, I thank Eben Alexander for writing his story, because it has inspired me to write mine.

James P. Holmes

CHAPTER ONE

My Accident

From "Song of Myself"

by Walt Whitman

"All goes onward...and nothing collapses,

And to die is different from what anyone supposed, and luckier.

Has anyone supposed it lucky to be born?

I hasten to inform him or her it is just as lucky to die, and I know it."

It was the day after Christmas, 1980. I was twenty-three and living in a house in North Falmouth, Massachusetts, with my friend Robbie.

"Robbie, you cooking dinner tonight?" I asked him.

"Cook what? The fridge is empty. Besides, I cooked last night; it's your turn."

"How about pizza? It's Saturday night, and I don't feel like going shopping. Do you?"

"Naw, I'm sick of pizza," Robbie said.

The house that Robbie and I were renting was less than a quarter mile from the North Falmouth House of Pizza, and we probably ate there too often, in keeping with our bachelor lifestyle.

"Bobby-B's?" I asked, using our abbreviation for "Bobby Byrne's Pub."

"Sounds good. I'm gonna take a shower. Leave in a half hour?"

"Sure thing."

"It's your night to have cooked, so you're driving," Robbie quipped on the way to the bathroom.

"Okay with me. I don't want to ride in your piece-of-junk car anyway," I barbed back, knowing the pride he took in recently buying his first new car with his hard-earned money. The car was nothing flashy—a four-door sedan better suited for a family—but it ran like a top and was all his.

It was a short drive to Bobby-B's, which made it very convenient for us to go there. We could grab dinner, a couple of beers, maybe run into a friend or two. Besides the lack of food in our house, there was another reason I wanted to go to Bobby-B's on that particular night. Every time we went on a Saturday night, I would see the same, very attractive, girl. She didn't appear to be with anyone other than her girlfriends, and several times we had made longer-than-usual-eye contact across the crowded bar. If I saw her again, I was determined to ask her out.

Robbie and I got to Bobby-B's around seven; we ordered dinner and a couple of Buds in the bottle. *Ahhh,* there's nothing like that first sip of ice-cold beer, even when it's December and way below freezing outside. I finished my dinner, and, as I started on my second Bud, I scanned the room for the girl I hoped to meet. Nothing. Who knows? The cold winter weather may have kept her home. Or maybe she had a boyfriend, after all. *Oh, well.*

Over our second beer, Robbie and I got into a heated debate with the bartenders about which team was better, the Red Sox or Yankees. Robbie argued for the Yankees only because he liked to stir things up. It was two bartenders and me against Robbie, and he loved it. I knew he hated the Yankees, like any good New Englander, but he loved to argue.

At a lull in the argument, I felt that someone was watching me. I turned in the direction I felt the stare was coming from, and there she was—the girl I was hoping to meet. Our eyes locked momentarily, and I detected a faint smile on her lips.

I'd had enough baseball talk—it was December, for crying out loud—so I made my way through the crowd in her direction. As I approached her, I noticed she was well dressed from head to toe. She had on new Bean winter boots, stylish jeans, and a beige peacoat with a complementary scarf around her neck. She looked like she had just stepped off a page of an L.L. Bean catalog. She had clear, smooth skin, deep-blue eyes, and light blond hair. She was, perhaps, out of my league, but I had a feeling that there was something very special about her.

I made my way through the crowd until I found myself in front of her. I introduced myself and, seeing that her hands were empty, offered to buy her a drink, which she accepted. She asked for a beer, a "Corona no lime," to be exact. We small-talked above the din of the bar crowd, and I was liking this girl more and more. Not only was she pretty but, more importantly, intelligent and well spoken. To top it all off, she liked to drink beer. A big plus in my book!

After talking for a while, we reached that point where we both realized there may be long-term dating potential in the other person. We exchanged phone numbers and agreed I would call her to make a date for the upcoming New Year's weekend. I was excited to have met a young woman of her caliber. She was different, a step up from the women I usually dated. *Maybe this is what I need in my life,* I thought, *someone who would inspire me to work harder, take life more seriously, and plan a direction in life.* As I returned to my seat at the bar next to Robbie, who was still arguing baseball, I thought, *This has been a great night.* I had this strong feeling, down deep, that my life was about to change. It was, but not in the way I imagined.

~ December 27, 1980, 12:00 midnight ~

*R*obbie and I left the bar around midnight. Once outside, the moonlit night and freezing temperature were a sharp contrast to the warm and friendly atmosphere we had just left. All I could think about was the pretty face, blond hair, and captivating perfume of the sweet girl I had just met. As I got into my cold car for the drive home, I could still hear her gentle voice. Robbie and I sat in the car for several minutes, letting the engine warm up. But we were too cold to wait for the heat. Robbie looked at me and said, "What are you waiting for, man? We can drive all the way home before this damn car warms up. Let's go!"

The route home was easy. Take a left out of Mashpee Commons onto Rte. 151, follow it through one intersection at Sandwich Road, and continue all the way to the end at Rte. 28A. Then take a right at the light onto 28A, past the North Falmouth House of Pizza; our house was on the right, up about two hundred feet. Maybe a total of eight miles.

The police report states that my car skidded on a patch of black ice at the intersection of Rte. 151 and Sandwich Road. This caused my car to go off the road, out of control, and into the woods, running over small trees and brush until it hit a large and un-yielding pine tree.

It was late at night—actually early morning—and we were off the road, well into the woods. Some of the smaller trees and grasses we had run over sprang back up, combining with the darkness of night to cover the accident scene, in what seemed to be a conspiracy of nature to keep us hidden from any rescue effort. The engine died on impact, and the smashed battery could keep the head lights on only momentarily. They went from bright white to a brownish flutter to black. The sole beacon of light to alert anyone to our presence was extinguished.

How long we sat broken and bleeding in my car, no one will ever know. Doctors later speculated that the cold weather—zero degrees Fahrenheit, the same cold that caused the black ice to form—may have also saved Robbie's life, by helping to stem the flow of blood from his body.

A typical young, arrogant male, I never wore my seat belt. I thought I was invincible, and seat belts were not cool. So, when car met tree, my body became a speeding projectile. My head hit the inside of my car so hard that part of my brain was instantly pulverized, turning into liquefied brain matter. My skull fractured on impact, and broken pieces of cranium jammed into my brain. This severe head trauma caused blood clots the size of grapes to form in my brain. Numerous other broken bones and punctured organs severely affected my health, to say the least.

Robbie did not have his seat belt on, either, and his head and body also suffered similar damage, but less severe than mine. We were both unconscious, and neither of us would wake up for a long time. So, there we sat, completely helpless on an absolutely beautiful but bone-chilling cold December morning.

Head wounds always bleed profusely, and mine was no exception. My body came to rest in an awkward sitting position, partially slumped over the steering wheel. Blood poured out of a jagged gash along the right side of my head, starting a few inches above my ear and continuing across my forehead. The blood running out of my wound mixed with the pulverized, liquefied brain matter that was seeping out through my broken skull.

This ghoulish concoction proceeded to run down my face, over my lips, and down to my chin, where it formed large red drops that dripped to the car floor, creating a rapidly expanding pool of blood and brains. Blood passed over my parted lips, changing into frothy air bubbles, as my shocked and confused body instinctively tried to breathe. One of my lungs was punctured, and my brain was badly damaged. I needed air, oxygen. I needed desperately to breathe.

My body moved. The movements were minor ones, but at least something was moving. More pronounced movements followed. They weren't the deliberate efforts of an injured person trying to help himself, but rather the herky-jerky motions of severe muscle spasms, induced by a brain gone hay-wire. I was having a seizure.

As the seizure built in magnitude, my muscles responded accordingly. My legs were pinned in the car and could only tremble. My arms had a little more freedom, but the smashed cockpit restricted their range of motion. My head, however, was relatively free, and so it jerked violently from side to side, my jaws opening and snapping as blood from my head wound flew around inside the car. The seizure lasted only a few seconds, and then my body slumped back over the steering wheel.

Precious minutes went by. The dripping of blood off my chin slowed considerably—the chill December air was slowly robbing my body of what little warmth it had left. My heart continued to beat until a combination of factors started to disrupt its rhythm. Not enough blood caused the internal heart valves to malfunction. A falling body temperature made it harder and harder for my heart to beat, until it quivered in its final death throes. Then it just stopped.

The only sounds to be heard now were the occasional drop of blood splashing into the pool on the floorboards and the hiss of a radiator leak. Otherwise, there was only silence.

Then, far off in the distance, barely audible, was the siren of a police car.

I never met the young couple who found us. Not long after the accident, I was told who they were, but I was dealing with so much at the time that I have long since forgotten their names.

This is unfortunate. I really wanted to thank them. If not for the girlfriend's persistence that night, we surely would have died. I think the man's name was "Bobby," and I will call his girlfriend "Nicole." From what I was told much later, this is probably how the discovery of the accident scene played out that night:

The well-worn brake pads of Bobby's Ford Fairlane ground his car to a halt as he approached the stop sign at the intersection of Rte. 151 and Sandwich Road. Nicole sat next to him more for warmth than affection, as the heater in his aging car struggled to put out any heat at all. Before they moved on, the car's headlights reflected off something in the woods.

"What's that?" Nicole asked.

Bobby really didn't care. He just wanted to get home before the cops stopped him, again. It had been another hard night of partying at a friend's house, and he only wanted to climb into bed.

"Wait," Nicole persisted. "Look over there. Do you see it?"

Reluctantly, he looked in the direction she was pointing, fully expecting to see a reflector on a street sign or telephone pole. But even with bloodshot eyes and a slight beer buzz, he could tell that something was not right about the scene in front of him. With his curiosity now piqued, he drove straight through the intersection instead of taking a left toward home. He swung his car around and brought his headlights to bear on whatever was in the woods. First, they saw the tire tracks.

"Look, it looks like someone drove their car into the woods—see?"

Bobby turned the steering wheel slightly to the right to direct his headlights down the fresh car tracks leading into the woods. His eyes followed along a pathway of bent and broken small trees and bushes until they came to rest on the reflection of taillights. It was a peaceful but eerie scene that the headlights illuminated: car and tree joined, with a slight wisp of steam rising from the engine into the dark morning air. Their pulses quickened as they realized they had discovered a serious car wreck. The effects of drinking and smoking that night instantly left their brains. Adrenaline kicked in with the impulse to help another human being in trouble.

"I gotta go look," Bobby said, opening the driver's door and getting out.

"Be careful!" Nicole called after him.

From where she sat, all she could see was Bobby's back, with his familiar gait, walking away from her, the bent trees and matted grass pointing the way toward the bright taillights in the woods. Slowly, he approached the wrecked vehicle. The engine was not running, and the windows were up. He was just about to open the driver's door when he saw what looked like strawberry jam on the inside of the window. *Strawberry jam*, he thought. *That's weird. What would they be doing with strawberry jam?*

Something clicked in his mind, and he realized what he was looking at was human blood coagulating on the cold glass inside the car. Then he could see a head covered with what looked like *lots* of strawberry jam.

Reflexively, he jerked his hand away from the door handle. He had seen enough. He stumbled, trying to run back to the security of his car and girlfriend. Nicole watched as Bobby ran and tripped his way out of the woods.

Something's really wrong, she thought. *This is scary now.*

Back behind the wheel of his car, little beads of sweat broke out on Bobby's forehead.

"Bobby—what is it? What did you see? What's wrong?" Nicole had never seen her boyfriend of two years look so scared, so out of control of his emotions. Nothing ever bothered him. His silence was making her scared, and tears started to well up in her eyes.

"Bobby! What's wrong?" she pleaded.

"I think they're dead," he said matter-of-factly. "I think they're dead," he repeated in a much lower voice, almost to himself, as if confirming with his voice what he had seen with his eyes.

And he was right. I was dead.

"We have to go get help," he said. He put the car in drive, and sped away from the scene of the accident, yes to get help, but also to leave the gory scene well behind both of them.

It would take several attempts, banging on doors at one o'clock in the morning, until Bobby and Nicole found someone awake and willing to answer the door.

"Hi, I'm sorry to bother you so late, but there's a bad accident just down the road at the intersection, and I think they're dead," Bobby blurted out at two houses before the door was slammed shut in his face, as he expected.

At the third house, a man's sleepy voice said through the slightly opened front door, "What, what? Slow down; come in."

The house lights were flipped on and the invitation repeated.

"Come in, come in. Do you know what time it is?" the man asked.

"No, sir. I'm not sure of the time, but, you see, my girlfriend and I found this car wreck in the woods and I saw the blood and they're still in the car and we need to call the police."

"In the woods? What were you kids doing in the woods?"

"No, no, no. We could see the car in the woods from the road," Bobby replied, starting to get a little agitated. "We gotta tell the police."

"Phone's right over there—help yourself." And with that, the man sat back down in his worn recliner to watch the end of *The Tonight Show With Johnny Carson.*

Bobby called the police, told them about the wreck, and answered all their questions. He thanked the man for the use of his phone, and he let himself out the front door, pulling it shut behind him. As he stepped out into the cold air, he looked up at the bright morning stars, and he thanked God it was not Nicole and himself in the wreck they had both just left.

All this effort by the good Samaritans took time. Potentially, the seconds ticking away were the difference between living and dying for Robbie. As for me, the only hope was that the EMTs would be able to jump-start my already dead and slowly cooling body back to life.

Robbie's heart was still beating when the EMTs arrived. Having the best chance for survival, he was attended to first. Once cut from the wreckage by the "jaws of life," he was quickly stabilized and taken in an ambulance to nearby Falmouth Hospital. After he was on his way, the rescue crews turned their full attention to me.

The quiet of the early morning was once again interrupted by the jaws of life. It bit through or re-twisted already mangled metal and glass to allow access to my lifeless body. Their first priority with me was to try to restart my heart. Without a heartbeat, nothing else mattered. With my favorite shirt ripped open to expose my bare chest, the command of "clear" was shouted to alert everyone that paddles full of electricity were about to be applied to my chest in an attempt to jolt my heart back into action. As the paddles hit me, my broken and bloody body convulsed in an awkward spasm. The potentially lifesaving shock seemed to have an effect on every muscle in my body—except the intended target. There was not even a quiver from my heart. Too many essential things were wrong.

"Clear!"

The command once again sounded as the re-energized paddles headed for my chest. Another awkward body spasm, electricity tweaking the muscles of my upper torso—all but my heart.

This is it, pal, thought the EMT. *Three strikes and you're out!*

For the third time, "Clear!" was announced for all to hear.

Bam! The lifeless body contorted as paddles and electricity met skin—my skin.

My heart began to weakly beat again.

"We got him—we got him back!" shouted the EMT.

He was right. I was back. *But from where?*

CHAPTER TWO

My Life Before the Accident

In June of 1969, I was twelve years old. My parents made me and my four older sisters put on our good clothes and took us to church. The collar of my white dress shirt irritated my neck, and my clip-on tie refused to stay straight. It was a beautiful sunny Sunday morning, and I could think of a hundred other things to do than be in church, like: go fishing off the Green Pond bridge, play a pickup baseball game with my friends, or just watch cartoons on TV, to name a few. My father might have physically driven us to church, but guilt was the driving force that really got us there. My parents always went to the center aisle, where the usher would lead us down to our usual spot. We all sat in a pew three rows from the front, where it seemed the minister leaned over from the pulpit to preach directly to us, in all of our unworthy humanity.

As usual on a hot summer day, the windows of the white Congregational church were open, and the ceiling fan turned lazily in a failing effort to keep the parishioners comfortable. All it really managed to do was push around the hot and humid air. Occasionally a police car or fire truck would speed past with sirens blaring. No one could hear the minister above the noise, but he just kept talking, making me wonder if anyone ever really listened to him. All seven of us took up a full pew, but, sometimes, we were forced to squish together to accommodate a single churchgoer, usually an elderly woman who smelled like mothballs and wore makeup that appeared to have been drawn with crayons. Her bright red lips seemed out of place in church, and the blue around her eyes almost made me laugh out loud, having been applied by shaky hands directed by failing vision. My mother, noticing the odd look on my face, glared at me with an expression that said, without words, "Jimmy—don't stare. Be nice to your elders, especially in church. It is the Christian thing to do."

"Fine." I would just sit there and swing my feet, lightly kicking the back of the white wooden pew in front of me, just hard enough to leave black scuff marks from my uncomfortable church shoes. My rebellious act did not go on for long. I get *the look* from one of my sisters, but I don't stop until it comes from Mom or Dad. I really did not care. The whole church thing made no sense to me. Religion was very distant from my young life. Sure, I thought I might need it when I got old, like "Mrs.

Mothballs," but right then, I didn't get it, and I didn't need it. Besides, there was another church across the street, and yet another one just down the road, where the people who go there do different things to worship the same God. I thought, *Which one is right? Is there a wrong church to belong to? Are the people better in one church than another?* I had a lot of questions in my twelve-year-old brain, but the most pressing question that I had at that moment was "How much longer until church is over?" So, I sat there, wasting my childhood. The minister droned on about the Bible, the choir sang, and then the minister droned on some more.

After the service, my mother invited "Mrs. Mothballs" back to our house for Sunday dinner, where bits of food would collect at the corner of her mouth. Completely unaware of how disgusting she looked, she leaned toward me and said, "So, James. How are you doing in school? How old are you now?" and blah, blah, blah. All I could see is that stupid crumb at the corner of her mouth and how really old and cracked the skin of her face was. "Okay, fine. Twelve—and may I please be excused?" I asked my father. That was about the extent of my contribution to the dinner-table conversation. I had better things to do.

My parents often invited less-fortunate people over for Sunday dinner and all the holiday meals. I didn't like that. I did not like having people who were different from us at our table. One woman who always got invited for the holidays was *really* old, with crazy hair that stood straight up, and if *she* had smelled like mothballs, it would have been an improvement. To top it off, she always brought her son, who was mentally slow and reminded me of a balding, real-life Humpty Dumpty. He chewed his food with his mouth open, exposing yellow chiclet teeth that ground and smashed whatever was in his mouth until it was fit to swallow. I couldn't help but watch this train wreck of table manners, at our table, of all places. If I had done half of what he was doing, I would be sent to my room without dinner.

I just wanted our family to be together. Being the youngest of five children, I wanted more attention from my parents. It was already spread thin over the five of us, and the guests at our table only further diluted what my parents had to offer. I saw my parents doing the "right" thing for others, and I resented it. Deep down, I knew I was not really "the good Christian" the minister talked about in church, and I felt that a cold, black hole in the ground would be an upgrade from what I deserved when I was dead.

I once asked the parents of a good friend why they never went to church. His father said, in his humorous way, "I don't go because I don't want to sit in somebody else's pew, or mine either, for that matter!" He would chuckle at his play on words, but he never gave me a serious explanation, and, as far as I knew, they never went to church.

Church scared me to a certain extent. The overall message I got from it was that I was not worthy of Everlasting Life, whatever that was. I knew that it is different from life as I know it, and I cannot imagine it being better, only worse. I feared dying, and this inescapable eventuality kept me awake some nights. All I could think of was my body in a cold and dark hole in the ground—completely engulfed in darkness, with no sound and not even a pinprick of light for all of eternity. I felt trapped in life by my eventual death. I was really scared of dying, but there was no choice. I had a real problem with that.

~ Childhood ~

The town of Falmouth is on Cape Cod, that hook-shaped peninsula sticking out into the Atlantic Ocean. Known as "the Cape," it was formed approximately twenty-five thousand years ago by stone and earth, pushed along at the tip of a glacier that came to rest over the Eastern Seaboard and then melted away. What remained became the beautiful islands of Martha's Vineyard and Nantucket, and the Cape, known worldwide for its miles of sandy beaches and sparkling ocean views.

The youngest of five children, I was fortunate to be the product of a good family with a sound upbringing. My sisters tell me that when I was young, they adored me. I was funny, loved to laugh, and was "just a sweet, little boy." This birth order and happenstance definitely developed a sensitive and caring side in me at a young age. A possible byproduct of this sensitivity was a feeling of being connected to a higher being. I did not understand it, but an inner voice tried to direct me at times, especially when it came to decisions of right or wrong. The possibility that this voice might be God made me very uncomfortable, and the whole concept was too awkward for me to ever mention it to anybody.

Growing up, it seemed like I was sick all the time. I had asthma that hampered my breathing, along with allergies to dust, green mold, and dog and cat dander. I was miserable because of it, often laboring to breathe, especially in the cold of winter. I never went anywhere without my inhaler. It seemed I was always at a doctor's office, either trying to figure out what was wrong with me or getting injections for what they had found. My mother brought me to our local family doctor for weekly shots, and I had monthly appointments with an allergy specialist in the nearby city of New Bedford.

The allergy specialist instructed my mother to keep our house exceptionally clean. In an effort to keep the house free of allergens, she threw her heart and soul into keeping our home pristine, so her son could breathe comfortably. When I visited a friend's house, I was better off to play outside. Invariably while playing inside, I'd be triggered by something in their house, the sneezing fits would start, and then the wheezing and labored breathing. I was always the oddball, the one who had to leave early or go outside in the fresh air to breathe and wait for a ride home. Because of this, I developed a complex and felt inferior. I felt like I was always dragging other people down for health reasons that were out of my control.

One night in particular sticks out in my mind, as it portrays how my health issues not only limited my ability to have a good time but also affected the happiness of others. Peter was my best friend growing up, and his parents had a "camp" up in Maine. They always invited me to go with them, and the way they talked about the cabin and surrounding woods made it sound like a great time. After repeatedly being asked to join them, I reluctantly accepted their invitation — "reluctantly" because I did not like to go places I was not familiar with, especially if I had to sleep there. As soon as I stepped foot into the camp, I knew I was in trouble. I could smell the dog dander (they had a beagle named Patches who slept wherever he wanted), and mold and dust were thick in the stagnant air. The place was opened up maybe only once a month, and the infrequency of opening a door or window for air circulation made the situation worse. The cleaning was below par for my condition, as dust was everywhere. I tried to relax but knew what was coming. I spent as much time outside as possible, but as darkness fell and dinner was served, I had to go inside.

Everyone else was fine and oblivious to my labored breathing, until I really started to wheeze. I asked to be taken to a motel. I told them their camp was too dirty for me to stay in. But I was just a kid, too young to stay in a motel by myself, and I had no money to pay for it. They were understandably insulted and told me they would cut their weekend short, and we would go home in the morning. I was not asking for much. I only wanted to breathe easily, like everybody else.

I remember that night clearly. It was fall, and I opened the window next to my bed so I could breathe in the crisp night air. I actually moved my bed right under the only window in the room and propped my head on the pillows so my nose and mouth were right on the windowsill, where I could drink in every breath of cold air like it was my last. My friend was sleeping in the other bed in the room and complained about being cold; he asked me to please shut the window. He might as well have been asking me to slit my own throat. The results would have been the same.

I lowered the window as far as I could and still be able to inhale the clean night air. I was struggling to breathe, so I couldn't shut it all the way. The next morning was the worst. I woke up breathing better because of the open window, but I was the reason for my friend's family cutting their fun weekend short. I apologized, and they said it was okay. But I could see in their eyes what they thought of me.

It was really embarrassing, struggling with my health but having to appear like I was fine. I felt inferior to everyone else. It would have helped me tremendously if someone had said, "It's okay. I understand what you're going through." These invisible health issues would shadow me for the rest of my life. I pulled away from my friends. I was tired of trying to explain why I had trouble breathing. It was easier for me to stay home by myself — which meant, conversely, around my mother. She was a religious person, often singing hymns in the living room while playing the piano, a habit she picked up from her mother. I was young and impressionable, and I soaked it up.

My mother was the catalyst for my first breakthrough of communicating with God. I clearly remember a day when I felt overwhelmed with my life's problems. I couldn't solve them, and my family or doctors couldn't, either.

"Pray," my mother advised. "Pray to God, and tell him you're overwhelmed. Put your problems in God's hands. Then you can let them go."

I wasn't even sure I believed in God. In fact, talking about God or Jesus made me uncomfortable. In a way, I felt guilty praying to an entity I wasn't really sure I believed in. It seemed disingenuous. But I had nothing to lose.

With my eyes closed tight, I did just what Mom told me to do. As this was my first time praying to God to help me with my problems, I proceeded to pray an awkward but heartfelt prayer. I really wasn't expecting much, but when I was done and opened my eyes, the sensation was amazing. I could almost physically feel the burden being lifted from me. All from a simple prayer! This experience made a lasting impression on me.

This was the first of many times in my life when I knew that God was there for me. My problems were not solved, but I didn't feel alone with them. I just *knew* that things would get better and my problems would be worked out in due time—with

God's help, of course. This was the beginning of my off-and-on spiritual journey with God. Little did I know that, in my lifetime, I would briefly exist in death, as my spirit, in God's presence.

My father was strict but also inspiring. A tough role model to live up to, he took good care of himself, eating right and exercising. He was painfully disciplined. If Mom put a plate of cookies on the table for dessert, Dad would take one—literally, one. He was stern in the discipline of his children and pretty much viewed the world as black and white, right or wrong. There was little-to-no gray area in his way of thinking.

I would say, as I reached for another cookie, "Dad, aren't you going to have more?"

"No, that's enough for me. I don't want to get fat."

One cookie is enough? You have got to be kidding me, I would think. But that was Dad. His simple and frugal lifestyle was probably dictated by living through The Great Depression of the 1930s and the sacrifices of those who served in WWII.

~ Teenage Years ~

Given my asthma and allergies, I was lucky to have a father who, once he had children, made healthy living a priority. Dad loved to smoke a pipe, and I loved the smell of burning tobacco. Half and Half was Dad's tobacco of choice. The smell of burning pipe tobacco reminded me of family camping trips to Sebago Lake in Maine. Dad kept his pipes in a semi-circular pipe rack on his desk. Occasionally, I'd pull one out of the rack and despite the awful taste, pretend I was smoking a pipe. One day I told my father, "I can't wait to be old enough to smoke a pipe like you." Dad quit smoking that night— "cold turkey," as the saying goes. He threw out all of his pipes, and the pipe rack, too. I was impressed that he would give up something he enjoyed so much for me. I actually felt a little guilty, but Dad had made up his mind, and that was that.

Dad always believed physical fitness was important to a healthy and happy life. With his history of smoking pipes—and smoking a pack of cigarettes a day in the 1940s—he felt that it was time to "clean out" his lungs. So, he started to run. I saw what my father was doing and decided that I should run, too. At first, I ran back and forth on the sidewalk in front of our house. I was a chubby kid with pink cheeks and wheezed the whole time. As hard as it was, every time I finished running (actually more like a fast walk, initially), I felt good, and as time went on, the same route became easier. I liked the sore muscles earned by physical exertion, and the sweat and the sense of accomplishment earned by completing longer and longer runs. I also liked when people commented, "Oh, so you're a runner." As I lost weight, my body became toned. Instead of feeling ashamed of a body that could not complete the simple task of breathing without difficulty, I was now running miles at a time, breathing easy, getting in great shape, and improving my self-esteem. For a while Dad and I ran together, but as time went on, I needed to run faster and further than our two-plus-mile route. I had become obsessed with running.

This newfound passion, and my recollection of struggling to breathe with my asthma and allergies, kept me from smoking anything, ever. I hated the feeling of having to fight to breathe, as I had done for most of my young life. I was all done with that.

As cool as smoking looked, or seemed to be, I chose wheeze-free breathing. For me, it was not a difficult choice to make.

I remember runs down the Shining Sea bike path with my parents, some of my sisters, a brother in-law or two, and various family friends, really more of a jog, so we could stay together, laugh, and enjoy each other's company. Running was just something that my family and friends did. We talked pros and cons of different running shoes, how far we'd run, and what hurt. We laughed and joked as puddles of sweat formed beneath us as we sat on the back patio replenishing our bodies with cool glasses of water. My parents had put an old claw-foot bathtub in the herb garden in the backyard, and there was nothing better after a long run on a hot day than filling the tub with cold hose water and immersing yourself in it. The coolness of the water, the smell of fresh herbs, and the gentle buzz of honeybees collecting pollen all made for a peaceful and serene experience. Life was good.

In school, I was a shy kid with average grades; my teachers were always trying to coax out the potential they knew lay untapped inside. But I was content to just get by. If I tried harder, my reasoning went, I would only expose myself to mistakes, receiving criticism and ridicule in return for sharing my ideas and thoughts. So, I chose to exist in the protective shadows of mediocrity.

During sophomore year in high school, a classmate of mine, who knew that I liked to run, told me the soccer team really needed players. I knew nothing about the sport, but my friend David was pretty insistent that I at least try out.

"C'mon, Jimmy," he said, "we don't win much, but we have a lot of fun." He named all the people I already knew who were on the team. I was afraid to fail. I didn't want to let down or limit anyone else in my life because of my breathing problems—which, by the way, were by then well under control because of my running—but I was still reluctant to try out. With David's encouragement, I eventually tried out for the team. And to my surprise, I made the roster. I quickly learned the sport and was eventually recognized by my coaches as a leader and a hard worker. It was a proud moment when I became an all-star and was elected team captain my senior year.

This part of my past is all well and good, but most importantly, the precedent of staying physically fit had been firmly ingrained in me. This healthy habit, the same one that allowed me to breathe easier through my respiratory challenges as a child, would, in the not-too-distant future, help to save my life.

~ After High School ~

As I grew into a young man, my shyness and lack of interaction with other children (because of my asthma and allergies) manifested itself in an awkward way. I seemed to lack a certain element in my makeup, or it just could have been a lack of discipline, but I always looked for the easy way out of a situation or relationship, consequences be dammed. I avoided confrontation. I would rather let relationships fade away than deal with it face to face. I didn't have what it took to tell a girlfriend that our relationship was over. *Just don't answer the phone,* I would tell myself. *Ignore the knock on the door. They'll go away eventually, their tears will dry on their own, and life will go on.* This type of avoidance was a huge character flaw, and I knew it. I felt I wasn't much of a man inside.

My best friend Peter went on to a four-year college in Maine. Upon graduation, he started his career working in management for some of the largest paper companies in the world. My path in life could not have been more different. After graduating from high school with average grades, I attended three different colleges over a period of four years: Clark University, the Great Lakes Maritime Academy, and lastly, Wentworth Institute of Technology in Boston. I was smart enough to get in, but I lacked the work ethic and discipline to stay. Not succeeding at college bothered me, but not enough to make me buckle down and get serious with my education. I was not volunteering or helping others. I did not know what I wanted to do, much less making a plan to get there. Nope, not me. I was content to go with the flow. Hardly a life that God would notice, and certainly not one worth bringing back from the dead.

I was also different because I had spent so much time alone as a child. I had adjusted to this circumstance by not needing other people. I was content to be by myself. Having developed this aloof mannerism, I was always misunderstood. People my age and their parents would say that I acted as if I were superior, as if I thought I was better than everybody else. This was ridiculous! I never felt that way. In fact, I lacked self-confidence. This misconception made me draw further back into my shell. I was simply a quiet person who liked to keep to myself—a loner.

For several years, during and after high school, I worked as a deckhand on a ferry boat between Falmouth Harbor and Oak Bluffs on Martha's Vineyard. It was one of the "cool" places to work in town, and you had to "know somebody" to get a job there—it was my father's reputation as a good person and businessman in town that got me the job. The best part of the job was seeing and meeting all the summer girls going to and from Martha's Vineyard. On a hot summer's day, the top deck would be crowded with girls working on their tan, dressed to maximize skin exposure to the sun. What more could a young man ask for?

I had a girlfriend at the time, Wendy, who was a lifeguard at Falmouth Heights beach, just down the street from the harbor where I worked.

Wendy and I met at a dance bar called On the Rocks, just over the Falmouth town line in Mashpee. She was there with a bunch of her lifeguard friends, and I went with my friend Peter, whose uncle owned the place. It was a seasonal bar, catering to a young summer crowd with live bands, cheap drinks, and lots of room to dance.

I went to high school with one of the lifeguards who Wendy was with. Seeing David talking with a pretty girl, I took the opportunity and went over and sat down at their table, hoping he would introduce us, which, after some prodding, he did. Wendy and I liked each other immediately. The band started back up; the music was too loud for conversation, so I leaned in and asked Wendy to dance, an invitation she readily accepted. We danced the night away, and, when it was time to go home, we made plans to do it again soon.

Wendy and I had a lot of fun together, but every fall she had to go back to classes at Boston College, and I stayed in town to work. At first, we made the separated relationship work, until it just proved too hard for both of us, and we decided to break up. But, come summer, we always got back together again. This off-and-on relationship would continue for years.

As the saying goes: the world was my oyster. I had a great job, lived in a beautiful place, was handsome and athletic, with deep blue eyes, topped off by a full head of curly, light-brown hair. The problem was that I didn't like myself. I did not like the person I was turning into. I was torn between the thoughtful, sensitive boy I used to be and the hard-drinking, insensitive male all my new friends seemed to admire. That type of person wasn't who I was, but I tried to be like that in an effort to fit in. I privately wished for a life-altering event to set me on the right course, to wipe my "life slate" clean, to give me a "do-over."

I knew when I was doing something wrong, I was very aware of it. My inner voice always tried to stop me, and I had to work hard to ignore it. It could be lying, entering a relationship I had no intention of taking seriously, or just being mean to someone. Deep down I always knew I was doing the wrong thing. Once or twice would have been acceptable—we all make mistakes— but, as time went on, and the same actions were repeated, the guilt built up inside of me. It was this cumulative effect of my behavior that was starting to drag me down, as the joy of life was slowly leaving me. I was not growing into the man that I should be, and I knew it.

I didn't belong in church. I felt incapable of leading the righteous life that the Bible demanded. I had broken too many commandments to ever be worthy of God's salvation. I didn't belong with my new friends. I was trying to be something I was not, and my old friends had left me because of the person I had become. The "sweet little boy" my sisters once loved was buried deep within me. Good looks, an athletic body, and some money had turned me into a pompous ass with little regard for other people's emotions and feelings. Worst of all, I did not care. Or so I told myself. There was always that little voice inside, reminding me to make the right choice or do the decent thing, but I consistently ignored it.

Eventually, the voice got too loud and persistent. My life was going nowhere, and I knew things had to change—no, *I* had to change. But how? At twenty-three, I had repeatedly blown my chance at a college education my parents would pay for. I now had a good job with a local construction company, but I kept making the same moral mistakes. I was my own worst enemy, and I could not see a clear way out of the mess that I continued to make of my life, as well as of the lives of others.

I remember lying in bed at night thinking that, if I were in a car accident and was hurt badly—a head injury, to be more precise—all my past mistakes would be forgiven. I could then start life over. Instead of owning up to the position I had put my life into, I was looking for someone or something to do it for me. Once again, the easy way out.

This poorly thought-out plan to change my life has always bothered me. Did I bring my accident upon myself by visualizing it? If so, what power had I tapped into to make such a thing happen? Was the accident God's answer to my unintentional prayer? Whether I caused it or not, my scheme to change my life played out almost exactly as I had hoped for. I was in a car accident and suffered a major head injury. It would change my entire life.

Be careful what you wish for. Truer words have never been spoken.

CHAPTER THREE

A Glimpse of Heaven

I died on a cold December morning, at twenty-three years of age. It was nothing like I thought it would be or could ever have imagined. Even though my car crash was violent, I did not die a violent death. The physical result of the crash was numerous broken bones and punctured organs. As I sat in my wrecked car, the pain must have been overwhelming. But I did not die a painful death. As a matter of fact, I felt nothing at all, and, in that state of numbness, I entered the first phase of dying.

When you are more dead than alive, some earthly things still cling to your remaining consciousness. Your experience on earth is all that your brain knows. When the brain ceases to function, all that it has known dies with it.

I recall three distinct stages that my brain—and then my spirit—entered and passed through: dying, being dead, and coming back to life.

~ Dying ~

Exact Time Unknown

My spirit emerged and left my body, which sat crumpled and broken in my car. Once free of my dying body, my spirit went to my sister Susan's old bedroom, in a house that my parents once owned on Main Street in Falmouth. Why my spirit went to this particular room, in this house, I have no idea.

One possibility is because, back in the 1930s and 1940s, this house had been owned by Dr. Thomas A. Wiswall. He was the typical family doctor of that time period. My mother recalls being told by a neighbor that the doctor was quite opinionated and would talk to anyone who would listen, a real character around town. Even so, he was best known for his compassion toward his patients, some of whom would make the trip from Martha's Vineyard to be treated by him. He would often let his patients from the island stay in his house while they were in his care.

One of the rooms where patients could stay was my sister Susan's. The closet in this room had plumbing, and at one time a sink, which my parents removed during renovations. I have always felt that there was something special about that closet, but I have no idea what or why. Maybe my spirit went to this room because so many sick patients of Dr. Wiswal had come there to be treated. The room represented a safe place, where his patients were not alone in their suffering. They could relax, knowing that they were under the doctor's care. This is total speculation on my part. I had never had strong feelings one way or the other about this room, but it is where my spirit went while I was dying.

My first recollection of dying is my spirit being in the upper corner of this room, where wall meets ceiling, to the left of the closet door. My spirit was in the center of what I can best describe as a flower, like a rose with all the petals forming ridges around the center, which is where I was. I do not know how to explain this, but I felt that I was nestled in love in the center of this "flower," and that is where my spirit existed. The center of this "flower" was white, glowing, and the surrounding petals were various shades of blue and purple. The "flower" was not perfectly round; it was more oval. From my spirit's vantage point in the center of the "flower," I looked down on myself, my body, lying in my sister's beautiful antique brass bed.

What I remember of my spirit being in the center of the "flower" is odd. It was not my body or even my head, but from my spirit I could see—which is a human trait, to be able to see. I could see the whole room, but my focus was on my body in the bed, just below my spirit. My body was not the broken, cold, and dead one slumped over a pool of blood and brains in a smashed car on the other side of town. This body below my spirit was whole, clean, warm, and at peace.

This is what my spirit saw: I was lying on my back, centered in the bed, with both arms by my sides. My legs were out straight as well, and just slightly parted. My body was delineated by the very neat summer bed linens covering me. My head was perfectly cradled by two pillows, one on top of the other. All in all, a serene picture of me at rest.

My spirit then left the "flower" in the corner and entered my body in the bed. I was now seeing the room from my body in the bed, just as if I were alive and everything was normal. From my position in the bed, I could see that it was a beautiful summer day, complete with rays of sunlight streaming through *all* the windows, as if the sun were shining all the way around the house. The windows were open about a foot, allowing the warm summer breeze to circulate through the room, gently waving the linen curtains and ever so lightly caressing my face. Lying in that bed was the epitome of rest, and all of my senses were experiencing only beautiful and peaceful feelings. After being washed, the bed linens had been hung on the clothesline in the side yard to dry. They had done more than dry; they had captured the essence of summer in every fiber, the warm breeze, the sunshine, the laid-back pace of a hot and lazy summer day— it was all there. I could smell it! One of the clearest things that I remember is the pattern on the bed sheets: The sheets were white, with forest green circles on them. The circles were all about eight inches across and lined up perfectly, both horizontally and vertically.

I could also see the gentle movement of the linen window curtains. They were light beige in color and made of a very light, almost transparent material. The curtains were so light in weight that it took only the slightest of summer breezes to move them, as the air came and went through the open windows. I also saw the neatness of the bed I was lying in. The sheets were turned down eight inches or so over the summer bedspread, which was smooth, with no wrinkles, except where the outline of my body was. Everything was in order. I could relax and be at peace knowing that everything was as it should be; there was nothing left for me to do; it was okay for me to sleep. I could hear the lazy sounds of summer, the gentle rustling of the linen curtains, the occasional song-bird perched in the maple tree just outside the windows, a car slowly passing by. All of the right sounds, smells, and feelings were present to make for a perfect summer day on Cape Cod, the type of day when you crawl into bed for an afternoon nap, knowing that all is right with your world. You are free to sleep; there is nothing else that you should be doing. And so, I did. This is the path that my spirit took to leave this world—a path of light, beauty, and summer.

~ **Death** ~

A path of light, beauty, and summer led me to …

Imagine a galaxy of immeasurable dimensions slowly turning

on its axis, huge, majestic, and humbling in size. Upon close inspection, if you could, you would see a small spot of gold amongst all the brightly shining stars, all slowly turning in unison. That speck of gold, hardly discernible, was me.

Before I was born, as I rested in my mother's womb, my heart instinctively began to beat, a miracle unto itself. After twenty-three plus years of beating strong and healthy, mixed signals from my severely damaged brain and a cooling body cavity proved to be too much, and the instinct within this most vital of all muscles ceased to exist. My brain, even though damaged, continued to "live" on. However, as the flow of blood containing vital gases for my brain to function ceased, my brain died as well. I was dead.

All remnants of life were extinguished from my physical being. When my brain died, all that it "knew" died with it, and my spirit was completely released from my body. I was now pure energy, existing solely as my spirit. And my spirit went to my "gold spot" in the magnificent "galaxy of souls." This is where I belonged.

My journey was over. I was truly home.

I blended into this great community of souls—the vast galaxy—taking my rightful place among them. There was no "flower," no brass bed, or beautiful summer day. That had been in my dying phase, while my brain still functioned on some basic level, and my existence was portrayed to me by things my brain had experienced in my lifetime.

When I was dead, the connection to my past on earth was not defined by memories. That is impossible. Rather, the connection is that intangible emotional asset that we accumulate, and give off, while alive: Love.

While I was dead, my family and friends were with me as their love. Their past and present love was abiding with me, and I knew that their future love would continue to make its way to me, further expanding my "home" in the galaxy and comforting me. I would exist throughout eternity with their love surrounding me. Love has no boundaries. It is limitless and everlasting. Knowing that this is how we exist in death takes away the fear— the dark, black finality of death that I used to envision.

Love was all I brought with me from my past to my "gold spot," and it was all I would ever need.

In death, I was aware of a sense of the present (a feeling of joy, contentment, belonging) and also of a sense of the future (being where I am supposed to be through eternity). It is this sense of a past (love), a present (home), and a future (belonging) that makes death a dynamic phenomenon—opposed to the idea of it as a static existence, of a cold, dark, in-the-ground, one-dimensional death.

Knowing this to be true, I could live contently, without worries about death.

After being so smashed and broken in my accident, I should have suffered great pain. To the contrary, as I mentioned, I felt nothing. The only pain I experienced would be later, in this world, as I went through recovery, with all my fractured ribs. I actually felt guilty about this, about having a painless death. I had put my family and friends through so much sadness and fear for my well-being. I believed that I should have suffered more. But death isn't like that. Just as I don't remember suffering pain when I was born, I didn't suffer when I died.

Sometimes I have visions of when I was dead. In them, I am back in a limitless dimension, and my space in the galaxy of souls is available to me. From my "gold spot," I can reach out with my arms and grasp light years of distance and space. I am free again, with limitless space around me. It is a fantastic, wonderful, peaceful feeling. I was one with everything when I was dead, and the enormity of "everything" is beyond comprehension. It is limitless and timeless, but, most of all, it is love.

In retrospect, from my once-again-living brain, it is this sense of belonging that gives me the most comfort in knowing that I am going to eventually die, again. Dying was as natural and effortless as breathing, and it was where I was supposed to be.

I was home.

~ Coming Out of Death ~

As my body and brain started to function again on some basic level, my spirit went back into the "flower" in my sister Susan's room. This time, however, it was a dark and cold day. No sunlight was streaming through the windows, no summer breeze gently moving the linen curtains back and forth. Everything had a brown tinge to it. This was the same room that had been so beautiful and inviting. How could this be? As my spirit watched from the "flower," my body got out of the bed on the right side, the side closest to where the "flower" was. As I went to get out of bed, I flung back the nondescript bed linen to expose the white and green bed sheet in its entirety. This sheet was the only color in the room and left a tremendous impression on me.

When I later told a friend of the family (who was a minister) about the sheet, he suggested that the white of the sheet represented the light of God, the green in the circle was nature and life, and the circular shape represented eternal life. This explanation made so much sense to me that I have never bothered to explore the possibility of it meaning anything else.

As my body stood up, my spirit left the "flower" for good and was now back in my body. I walked around the end of the bed. There was another door in the room that led directly to the front hallway and staircase. It would have been much quicker for me to leave the room that way. But I ignored the quicker way out of the room and chose to take a left and walk along the side of the bed, which would lead directly to the other door and into the hallway. As soon as I made that left turn, everything changed. I could barely walk, I was cold and miserable, and everything in the room had turned a deeper shade of brown. I struggled to move. I could only shuffle my feet in an attempt to walk. It was as if my body was wrapped in chains and I was trying to walk through a thick brown mud up to my neck. The mud was cold, so very cold, and so was I.

As I shuffled along by the side of the bed, I looked down, and my body was back in the bed—my dead body. The summer day was back, filling the room with all its splendor. The bed with me in it was once again beautiful, comfortable, warm, and smelled like summer.

That is where I so desperately wanted to be, not freezing cold and struggling to walk. But I was given no choice. I had to continue on my way past the bed, and, as I did so, I was constantly looking down at my body with envy. I was finally past the bed and through the door and into the hallway, where I stood still, my back to the linen cabinets. The door I had just passed through was now on my right side, and it was closed. I had something like a black shawl around my shoulders for warmth. But I let it slip and fall to the floor. I could sense that I was not alone in the hallway—it appeared as if a person made of black smoke was next to me, on my left side, in an aggressive posture. Its face was very close to my face. Whatever it was, it seemed angry that I was leaving its control. This smoky figure slowly and fitfully shrank away, until it disappeared in the floor beneath my feet, as if being pulled through the wood floor by a vacuum—it did not leave voluntarily. And with that, it was over.

My spirit was back in my body. It was no longer residing as pure energy in the nest of love in the center of the "flower." My spirit needed to be condensed and found itself in unfamiliar territory, having to coexist with my human brain again. Even though they had existed together before, things were different now. My brain was badly damaged and could barely take care of itself, much less an entire body. My spirit had known limitless freedom and a spiritual existence beautiful beyond words. And now my brain, which was having problems of its own, was once again in charge. But my spirit was not going to go away quietly.

~ **Alive Again?** ~

Life, if you could call it that, had returned to my body. I was alive enough that my spirit had to return to my body. Even though my heart was beating, a machine was doing my breathing for me. I was spiritually and physically alive, but for all intents and purposes, brain dead. I don't know if I was brain dead or not, and in my reading you do not recover from it.

Somebody or something would not let me die completely. I was ready to die—I had accepted my fate and was content with being dead. But some part of my being had made a choice—but how is that even possible? In the state I was in, it could not have been me. Was it simply the EMTs who refused to give up on me? Or had God intervened and saved me for a greater purpose? If so, what?

CHAPTER FOUR

In the Hospital

~ December 27, 1980, 2:00 a.m. ~

There is a dreaded middle-of-the-night phone call that no parent ever wants to get. But my parents got it, and it was about me. "Mr. Holmes? My name is Dr. Robert Weaver. I'm a neurosurgeon at Cape Cod Hospital. Your son, James, has been in a serious car accident. I need your permission to operate."

After the EMT got my heart working again, I was brought by ambulance to Cape Cod Hospital in Hyannis. This hospital was chosen because it had recently acquired a state-of-the-art CAT scan unit. This medical tool proved to be invaluable in helping doctors see the extent of the damage to my head.

The EMTs had done their job. We may have been on life support, but both Robbie and I were technically alive. Briefly, I had fractured my skull, pushing bone into my brain, cutting it. As the operative record—included as Appendix B—states: "Several large segments of bone that were comminuted and depressed were then elevated along with the major bone flap. As this was done, pulverized liquefied brain matter came forth in the epidural space from a rent in the dura." The surgeon also found "grape-sized collections of black blood" within my brain. All the bones in my face were broken, except my nose. My right shoulder was separated, and all my ribs on one side were fractured; one had punctured a lung.

As I was being wheeled out of the operating room after brain surgery, my vital signs crashed—both of my lungs had collapsed. I was wheeled right back into surgery, where a chest tube was inserted and my lungs "re-inflated." My vital signs stabilized. To further complicate things, I then contracted pneumonia—in both lungs.

The outlook for a complete recovery was dismal. The damage my body and brain had sustained in the accident was just too much. If, by some miracle, I did survive, it was expected that I would be partially paralyzed, with limited vision, due to the part of my brain that had suffered extensive damage. I was also down to one comparatively good lung to supply my body and brain with the all the oxygen it needed, not just to live but to heal from its injuries—in essence, for me to survive.

At one point, Dr. Weaver told my father that, if I had been

a smoker or my lungs had been impaired in any way, there would have been no chance for me to survive. All those miles of running and living a smoke and drug-free life were paying off in a way that I never could have anticipated.

In the ICU, I exhibited no signs of brain activity. I was on life support. The only positive thing was that my heart continued to beat, oblivious to the severely damaged body in which it resided.

Since 1968, the medical community defines "death" as when the *brain* ceases to function, not the *heart*. So, with this definition, I was still essentially dead. I had some undamaged organs inside of me, and the clock was ticking on the horrendously difficult decision my family would have to make.

When do you give up hope? What is the optimum time to harvest my good organs and in turn send happiness and hope to another family?

At the time of my accident, my sister Susan was living in Maryland, working for the Union Trust Bank in downtown Baltimore. She would drive up to the Cape every year and spend

Christmas with my parents, staying at their house. Around two o'clock in the morning on December 27, she was sound asleep in her old bedroom, on the antique brass bed that she loved so much, when the ringing of the phone woke her up. At first, she dismissed it as a wrong number and started to fall back to sleep. Then she heard a commotion in the house, and she wondered what was going on. She could tell that my parents were up and about, doing more than just using the bathroom. So, she got up, put on her robe and slippers, and went to see what was happening. One look at the somber expression on my parents' faces, and she immediately knew something was wrong. *A relative must have died,* she thought. *Someone old. It would be too bad, but not completely unexpected.*

Then Mom said, "It's your brother. He's been in a car accident, and they have to operate. Your father and I are going over to see him right now. You stay here by the phone in case anyone else calls. We'll call you when we know more." And, with that, they were out the door, gone into the darkness of an early December morning. As Susan lay back down in bed with the phone nearby, all she knew was that her brother had been in a car accident and needed surgery. *At least he's still alive*, she thought, *and the operation was probably for a broken leg or something. He'll be alright.* The possibility of liquid brain matter coming out of my broken skull being the reason for surgery never crossed her mind.

My parents arrived at the hospital at about three thirty in the morning. Their arrival being anticipated, a nurse met them at the door and walked them to the family waiting area. I was being wheeled out of surgery when they arrived, and it just so happened that the corridor they were in was also used to get me to the Intensive Care Unit. My parents saw me being wheeled out of surgery, but it could have been anyone—clean bed linens hid my body, and white bandages covered my head and face. There was nothing to recognize, nothing for them to call their own. Then they and everyone else heard the alarms go off on my monitors as my vital signs crashed. There was a sharp command and sudden flurry of activity, and my parents watched me disappear back through the emergency operating room doors.

Then my parents were told that the person being wheeled back into surgery was their son. No explanation could be given to them, because nobody knew for sure what had just happened. But it did not take a medical degree to see that things did not look good for me. As it turned out, my body basically gave up, and both of my lungs had collapsed. And so, my parents did all that they could do: wait, shed tears about the unknown, and pray.

Dr. Weaver was a very talented brain surgeon and a man of few words. He took great pride in his work, and he took each patient he operates on as a personal challenge. And he hates to lose. He liked brain surgery. It was fairly straightforward. Just do your educated best to fix what was wrong with the patient's brain, nice and simple. Everyone in the operating room is an essential part of his team, with a specific job to do. Each person is focused on their job, with little talk other than the request for an instrument or the report of vital signs. And the patient, the focus of all this attention, is, of course, silent, no complaining, idle chitchat, crying, or dumb jokes. This is how Dr. Weaver liked it—a complete and concentrated effort in near silence, where he could intensely focus and do what he does best: operate on the human brain.

Dr. Weaver had seen brain injuries like mine before. Some

patients lived, but despite his best efforts, most of them died. The ones who lived were always permanently damaged, some far worse than others.

After hours of intense and meticulous surgery came the part that he disliked the most about his job: telling the patient's family about the condition of their loved one. He was spent, physically and mentally worn out by hours of standing, hunched over an operating table, trying to put the broken pieces of a young man's life and body back together. After removing his bloody scrubs and a quick splash of cold water on his face to refresh him, it was time to confront the family with the news of just how bad off their son was. Most importantly, he had to make sure he did not get my parents' hopes up. He told them that, despite his best efforts, it was more than likely I would not survive. If, by some miracle, I did live, I would never be the same person they had known.

Alone, afraid, and fearing the unknown about the condition of their only son, my parents waited quietly, not moving or talking for what seemed like hours. In their state of shock, they did not hear Dr. Weaver walk up to them or his first attempt to get their attention. He raised his voice just enough to penetrate the fog of incomprehension he knew they were existing in.

"Mr. and Mrs. Holmes?"

Both sets of tired and anxious eyes looked up with eager expectations about the condition of their son.

"I am Dr. Weaver, and I have just operated on your son …" He proceeded to deliver short and concise verbal punches that rocked my parents to their core. They sat still and unbelieving on the cold vinyl seats of the chairs in the family waiting area, dazed by what he told them. They listened to all he said, but all they heard was "severely brain damaged, collapsed lungs, not breathing on his own … probably will not survive."

Disbelief and denial were their gut reaction—all this could just not be true.

Are you sure you have the right person? they wanted to ask him. *There must be some mistake. Our son is healthy as a horse. We just saw him yesterday. He was fine.*

Slowly, Mom and Dad turned their heads to look at each other.

Their look said: *This cannot be happening to us, to him.* No words were spoken—it wasn't necessary. They each knew what the other was thinking. But it *was* happening to them. Every parent's worst fear had become reality. Their child lay broken in a coma, on life support, with little chance of surviving. The shock began to wear away, and it started to sink in. They held each other's hand. Tears ran down my mother's cheeks. Dad stared straight ahead, still trying to understand what they had just been told.

After his brief and factual talk, Dr. Weaver turned and walked away. He was exhausted after hours of surgery, putting what was left of their son's brains back into his head. When Mom and Dad could think again after being paralyzed by the devastatingly bad medical report, they at first felt helpless—useless. Overnight, so much had gone wrong and needed fixing. And the hardest part of the whole situation was that there was absolutely nothing that they could do about it. At a loss for what to do, my parents prayed for me, for my recovery. But it seemed like a pathetic attempt to help me. My skull was smashed, my body broken, and my brain badly damaged—and *praying* was all that they could do? Praying for me to live seemed like a bad prayer—living with brain damage could be a far worse life sentence for me than death. Praying for me to recover and be normal again seemed like asking for way too much. It just did not seem possible, with all that was wrong. All that was left to pray for was a miracle, and so that is what they did.

Mom and Dad slowly made their way to the hospital cafeteria. Not knowing what else to do, a cup of coffee seemed like a good idea. At that early hour, the cafeteria was empty.

The smell of fresh-brewed coffee was heavy in the air. No one was at the counter to take their simple order, but the banging of pots and pans in the back room assured them that someone would be out soon. When help finally showed up, Dad didn't know what to do. His mind kept seeing his son being pushed through operating room doors as alarms sounded everywhere.

"Sir, can I help you?" the pleasant voice repeated.

Brought back to the moment, he remembered, unfortunately, everything.

"Two cups of coffee, black please," he said, with no emotion.

"Two cups o' coffee coming right up; cream and sugar are on

the back table. Help yourself, sir."

Dad put money on the counter—how much he didn't know, nor did he care. He brought the cups back to the table where Mom was silently waiting. Dad sat down, took a deep breath, looked at the dark brown liquid in his cup, and felt more like throwing up than drinking coffee.

Mom looked into his eyes as if sensing the tension in his stomach. She reached out her hand and put it gently on top of Dad's clenched fist.

"Phil, look at me," she said sternly.

Dad lifted his tear-filled eyes to meet hers.

"Phil, everything will be all right. We will get through this together. We have to be strong for Jim. He needs us now more than ever." And with that, she gave Dad's hand a little squeeze.

This short talk gave both of them a direction, a purpose among the chaos.

"C'mon, Jean. We should call Susan and let her know." Dad's thoughts had turned from fear to action.

They got up and went to the courtesy phone in the back corner of the cafeteria. The night janitor was making his last rounds before his shift ended at four a.m. As he walked through the tables in the cafeteria, he noticed that all the tables were clean and ready for the day, just as he had left them an hour ago, except for one.

Coffee cups—dirty coffee cups? What the hell? People can't throw out their trash anymore? he thought.

He went to grab the first cup to toss into the trash, and he felt that it was still warm and full, untouched. The second one was, too.

Uh oh, he thought, *that's not a good sign.* Then he noticed the middle-aged couple at the phone holding hands.

"Damn," he said under his breath. He had heard of a kid brought in after a car accident earlier that morning. Rumor was the kid would not make it. He knew the signs of parents in distress over a child. He had been doing this job for too long and had seen it too often.

"God bless you—it looks like you're gonna need it," he said, tossing the full cups into the garbage.

Mom and Dad called Susan as they said they would, though not really sure what to say. Dad listened as the phone seemed to ring forever. Susan finally answered.

"Hello?" squeaked my sister's sleepy voice.

"Susan, this is Dad." Then there was a long pause as Dad composed himself.

"Hello?" she repeated in a slightly stronger voice, thinking she recognized it as Dad's.

"Susan, your brother is hurt, really bad. He's on life support. They don't think he will make it." Then Dad lost his ability to speak.

Did I just hear what I thought I did? Susan wondered. And then she could hear Mom's voice in the background.

"Phil, give me the phone. Let me talk to her."

Dad gave her the phone as if he were in a trance. The act of having to tell someone else what was going on forced him to accept the reality of the situation. He felt like throwing up again.

"Susan, Susan honey, it's Mom."

Before she could continue, Susan cut her off.

"Mom, is it true?" The sleepy voice had been replaced by one of fear. She was already half crying. "What Dad said—is it true?"

"Susan, listen to me." Mom's was voice steady and firm. "Yes, your brother has been hurt badly, but he's still alive. He's in intensive care, surrounded by great nurses and doctors. They're all wonderful, and everything possible is being done to help him."

"Is he going to die?" my sister asked anxiously.

"No, absolutely not," Mom replied with conviction in her voice, refusing to accept what she had been told.

"Susan, your father and I are going to stay here a little longer, and then we will be home. He can't have visitors yet, so we'll be home once we know everything is alright."

"Okay, I'll be here," replied a subdued voice. But Mom had already hung up.

***

After the initial shock of the accident wore off, and the severity of my injuries was understood, a very cruel waiting game began. No one knew how long this game would go on, what the right moves were, or what the outcome would be. My family had been abruptly thrust into this game, naïve to the rules and equipped with only the most rudimentary of tools: Love, hope, and faith.

Their opponent in this formidable game was a veteran player, with millions of victories to its credit, and more every single day: the callous indifference of Death.

The player making the winning move in this game would claim me as its prize, dead or alive. The other available prizes ranged between a brain-dead existence on life support, total paralysis, partial paralysis, loss of vision, or other such outcome. But Death was the heavy favorite. The possibility of me ever having a normal life again was as improbable as the rare royal flush in poker.

But my family had to play the hand they had been dealt in a game they wanted no part of. Their seemingly inadequate strategy against such overwhelming odds was to passively wait, pray, and then wait and pray some more. It was all that they or anyone else could do.

Every night, my sister and parents drove over to Hyannis to visit me in the hospital.

Dad would drive; Mom sat in the middle, with Susan on her right side. Little was said during the forty-minute drive, but there was not much to say. Words were not needed.

They drew strength from sitting so close to each other on the front seat of the station wagon. This was a family united in a common cause during the holidays—unfortunately, it was a tragedy that bound them together.

The Christmas gifts did not matter now, nor did the tree, the ornaments, the lights. What my family needed from one another could not be bought at a store, wrapped up with a pretty bow on top and placed under the tree. They all needed support, a shoulder to cry on, and, through their tears, tell a little story that went something like: Remember when Jimmy did this or said that? He was such a funny and happy kid.

The memory of past good times with me were all they had, and the tears would start to fall again when they realized I would not be part of any more family memories. The last memory they would have of me would be a hospital room, bandages covering most of my face and head, and machines keeping me alive. Every Christmas going forward would be scarred with thoughts of *This is the time of year that Jimmy died.* It was not some nondescript forgettable day in, let's say, September. It was two days after Christmas, and that holiday would hit my family like a sledgehammer year after year, reminding them of the first and youngest member of our family to die.

Every night when my parents and Susan visited me in the intensive care unit, they were always hoping for good news, expecting some positive change in me, anything to give them hope. For days, then for a solid week, I gave nothing back, not the twitch of a finger as my hands were held, no flutter of an eyelid to signal I was getting better, no sign at all to give my family the least bit of hope. I could not even draw my own breath. I lay perfectly still for days on end, the only noise in the room the slow and steady click of the ventilator breathing for me.

When Susan first saw me in the hospital, she had an overwhelming sense of acceptance. Nothing about my medical condition bothered her. My head was wrapped in bandages, white medical tape was over my mouth to hold the tubes running down my throat in place, multiple IVs were in my arms, and monitors were stuck to my chest. A small bottle was taped to the side of my head, with a tube going through my skull to drain fluids away from my brain, to reduce swelling. The blood and "what not" in the bottle were plain for all to see. She still does not know why, but upon seeing me, acceptance of my situation was the prevalent feeling that occupied her thoughts. She did not care about the blood, the bandages, and the lifeless body that was her only brother. She knew and accepted the fact that God was in control now, and she was at peace with the situation whether I lived or died.

As the one-week mark of me being in a comatose state approached, my father and mother were again told that my chances of survival did not look good at all. The only positive was my heart, which still kept beating. Other than that, nothing, not even a twitch. No response to familiar voices or the soothing touch of a family member holding my hand or foot. It appeared to everyone that I would live the rest of my life, however long that would be, in a comatose state. Everyone who knew me realized that I must be in hell on earth—that, if my brain was aware of anything at all, it would be the cruelest form of torture for me to be trapped in an unresponsive body. Letting me die would have been the merciful thing to do. What could be worse for the boy who loved to run along the ocean and hike in the Maine woods than living—if you could call it that—on life support in the sterile environment of an intensive care unit?

My parents were grasping for hope, for a miracle, for me. All that they had of me were memories. On one visit to the hospital, they were given my personal belongings: some salvageable clothes, my shoes, and wallet. In my wallet was my driver's license, with the required picture of me. This picture was special; not only was it recent, but it had *gone through the accident* with me, if that makes any sense. My parents now had something more viable to cling to, rather than a comatose, unresponsive body. A friend of the family took my license and had the photo blown up, framed, and placed by my hospital bed (see page 8). Part of me was now back for my parents, their smiling, curly haired boy in the picture could at least make eye contact, of sorts, which is more than could be said for me. The framed picture gave those who loved me something to believe in—hope for the return of *that* boy. To my family and friends, it represented the young man who they desperately clung to, as I teetered at the threshold of death. It represented all they had of me as they once knew me. If I did live—and it was a big IF—the boy in the picture would most likely never be back. No one knew what I would be like, mentally or physically.

The picture represented what my family knew, loved, and wanted back. A simple black-and-white driver's license picture, taken at the local Registry of Motor Vehicles, not known for their flattering photography, had become me.

<hr>

It was New Year's Eve, 1980. I should have been on a date with the girl I had met at Bobby Byrne's Pub the night of my accident. Instead, it appeared the only date I would ever be able to keep would be with my Creator.

New Year's Eve, a night of celebration around the world, to ring out the old, ring in the new. I always liked New Year's Eve because of the anticipation of a better year ahead, a starting-over point, to eat better, drink less, be a better brother, son, or friend. It is funny how circumstances change your perspective on what is meaningful in life. If I had been conscious that New Year's, I would have had a litany of resolutions that four days earlier would never have crossed my mind, such as resolving to walk again, talk again, and not have a machine breathe for me.

The whir and click of my ventilator and all the other machines keeping me alive would be my noisemakers for this New Year's Eve.

Mom, Dad, and Susan decided they would get dressed up and celebrate New Year's Eve in the hospital with me. It just felt like the right place to be. Along the way, they wanted to stop into a church to pray for me. My mother was getting really discouraged with my lack of response, and felt she really needed to talk to God in a place of worship.

It was a wet, cold, sleety, miserable December evening, with darkness having closed in earlier than usual because of the storm clouds gathered overhead. As Dad drove down Rte. 28 headed for Hyannis, they discovered that church after church along the way was closed. All they were looking for was a place to pray, a place of worship where they could feel more connected to God, a place where God would maybe pay more attention to their prayers. But every church along the route was as dark and uninviting as the winter weather they were driving through. My mother's heart sank to a new low. She was no longer asking for a miracle, just a church to pray in. She needed to know that God was paying attention to our family in its time of need. She was feeling lost and abandoned in her faith. Nothing was going right.

Even the cold and wet winter evening seemed to be against them.

When they finally got to the hospital, they hung up their wet overcoats in the visitors' area, which had become all too familiar to them. As usual, only two visitors at a time were allowed in the intensive care unit. That night, my mother could not bear to visit with me right away. It was too much for her. She was not ready to see her lifeless son again. No one's prayers were being answered. Even her simple request that a church be open had been ignored. She knew that, the longer I remained in a comatose state, the worse my chances for survival. It seemed like Death had won.

Mom was discouraged and felt defeated. She went into a quiet waiting room, where she could be by herself and collect her thoughts before seeing me. This particular room had a window that looked out over a wintry Hyannis harbor. Distant Christmas lights twinkled in the early-evening darkness as a cold December rain fell. It was a beautiful scene composed of miserable elements: cold, sleet, and a wintry darkness are hardly the components of what you would classify a beautiful winter scene, but all of this winter misery was offset by colorful Christmas lights decorating homes across the harbor.

I loved Christmas when I was a kid. The cold and snow made for a beautiful time of year. Mom would bake Christmas cookies that my sisters and I would decorate with a homemade sweet and colorful icing. On a special evening when Dad would get home from work, we would all pile into the car and go get our Christmas tree, always from the high school's Christmas tree lot.

I loved the smells of Christmas, the spruce Christmas tree, the baking cookies, and even the Christmas candle on the windowsill next to my bed. Christmas morning was always magical. I remember jumping up and down on my sisters' beds, shouting over and over, "It's Christmas morning, it's Christmas morning!" until they got up. Then we would run downstairs, and, there, under the tree, were what seemed like a mountain of presents—remember: there were five of us kids, so the "mountain" got pretty small once it was divided up. When they came downstairs, my parents looked exhausted—Dad from putting toys together late into the night, and Mom from wrapping presents and getting up early to put the turkey into the oven. It was a special time; it was family; it was fun.

Christmas had been the day before I crashed my car. It had been fun in the way that Christmases are fun with grown children: the magic is gone, but it's still great to see family and friends. We had gone, as a family, from the screams of delight as we ripped the wrapping paper off our gifts to the sobering reality of the impending death of one of us—me. The holidays would never be the same.

~~~~~~~~~~~~~~~~~~~~~~~~

Undaunted by the cold and sleet, Christmas lights pierced the darkness and made their way through the night, through the hospital window, all the way to my mother's tear-filled eyes. Here, in the waiting room, is where my mother prayed. It was not the church that she had hoped for, but it would have to do. She had something important to tell God. She did not pray for my recovery—it seemed to be too big of a miracle, even for God. I could not even breathe without a machine. I did not move or twitch a muscle, never mind talk or make eye contact. I
~~~~~~~~~~~~~~~~~~~~~~~~

gave nothing back to anyone, nothing to give them hope for my recovery. So, Mom prayed that I die peacefully, right now, end the worry and the torment that my family was going through, end my pain, end the suffering that she imagined I was in. "If there is a merciful God in heaven, please take him now; end this nightmare for all of us. Release Jim from his misery; release us from the constant tears and worry."

Mom had come to terms with the fact that her baby boy was just too broken, his injuries too overwhelming to realistically think I would live again.

So, my mother let me go.

She turned me over into God's hands, just as she had taught me to do with my problems so many years ago.

As Mom got up and turned away from the window, with tears running down her cheeks, she suddenly felt a warmth inside of her—a glow, as she described it—and, at that moment, she knew that God was there with her, making His presence known, letting Mom know that He had heard her prayer.

I was now in God's hands, and Mom took comfort in that.

The next day, I moved a toe.

When my family came to visit, the nurses had already turned back the blankets on my hospital bed to expose my feet, so everyone could see the big toe on my right foot occasionally move. Everyone was excited. There was lots of crying and hugging between family and hospital staff. Best of all, hope was back. I was still in a comatose state, but something, no matter how small, was working within my brain again. It now seemed possible that I could come out of my coma, someday. It was not much to look forward to, but it was something. It was a small pinprick of light—maybe a Christmas light—at the end of a very long and dark tunnel.

CHAPTER FIVE

Alive Again

~The Week of December 28, 1980 Through January 3, 1981~

*C*onsidering that hospitals are full of people, they are, for the most part, eerily quiet—the intensive care units even more so.

Anxious to see me after the big event the day before, me moving a toe, my parents made their way into my room. The blankets on my bed had been turned down again, exposing my feet in anticipation of their visit.

"Hi, Jim. Dad and I are here to see you," my mother said as she caressed one of my exposed feet in her hand. "Phil, say something to him and rub his other foot," she instructed Dad.

As he began rubbing my left foot, he said, "Hi, Jim—it's Dad. Your mother and I are here to visit you."

Dad was never good at small talk, and talking to a comatose person, even though I was his son, was way out of his comfort zone.

"Go on, Phil—tell him about your day. The nurses say it's important that we talk to him," Mom encouraged.

So, Dad went on for a little bit, talking about work and an upcoming Conservation Commission meeting where he had to make a presentation, occasionally glancing at Mom to make sure he was doing a good job.

"Jim, honey—it's Mom. How was your day today? I ran into Mrs. Eastman at the hardware store, and she asked how you were doing. The phone has been ringing off the hook with concern for you," and on she went, just casually talking to her son, like nothing was wrong.

Neither of my parents wanted to look at my toe that had moved the day before—they didn't want to see it *not* move. The previous week had been hard enough, and they didn't know if they could handle anymore disappointment. Then—

"Phil, I felt something! I think his toe moved again."

"You probably did," a deep voice said from the doorway. "It's been twitching all day."

So focused on their son, they had not heard Dr. Weaver enter the room.

"Oh, you startled me!" Mom exclaimed.

"Sorry—didn't mean to. I'm just making my rounds."

"So … Dr. Weaver, this is good? Is he coming out of his coma?" Dad asked.

"I'll be honest," Dr. Weaver replied. "It doesn't mean much. It could just be a muscle spasm. On the other hand, it could be the beginning of some brain activity. But don't get your hopes up," he quickly threw in. "Your son is in very bad shape." He added, "Medically, we have done all that can be done. Now it's up to Jim and God." With that said, he left the room.

Hardly comforting words, but it was the truth.

~ Marty and Gail ~

At the time, my oldest sister Marty was living in an apartment in Framingham, and she had just recently told my family she was gay. This news did not sit well with some members of my family, and Christmas in 1980 had been particularly hard, with mixed emotions and, to a certain extent, denial. We did not see Marty that Christmas, as the situation was too new and uncomfortable, nor did we get to meet her partner Gail. No one was happy with how this Christmas went. Everyone felt that we were family and that we belonged together, especially at that time of year. But the situation was too new, and we were all digesting the news, unsure of what to do. Marty and Gail did not want to upset the holidays for my family, so Marty decided to not come home for Christmas that year.

My sister Susan called Marty the morning of December 27. Marty answered her phone with a simple "Hello," wondering why Gail would be calling her so early.

"Marty, it's Susan," she bluntly stated.

There was a brief pause on the phone line as a surprised Marty understood who it was.

"Susan. Hi, how are you?"

"Marty, I'm not doing so well. Mom and Dad asked me to call everyone with some bad news."

Again, there was a pause from Marty's end of the line as a myriad of bad-news scenarios raced through her mind, none of which would prove to be correct.

"It's Jimmy," Susan blurted out, fighting back a sob.

"What? What do you mean, 'Jimmy'? Slow down, and tell me what's wrong."

"Oh, Marty, he's hurt really bad. He was in a bad car accident, and he's been in emergency surgery for hours," Susan was able to get out. And then her voice started to waver, with crying not far behind.

This time, there was a longer silence from Marty as she processed what she had just heard.

"Susan … Susan! I need you to talk to me. Is he still alive?"

"Yes, I think so," Susan replied between sobs.

"Okay, that's something; that's good. What hospital is he in?" Marty asked, thinking for sure I must be in one of the elite hospitals in Boston.

"Cape Cod Hospital in Hyannis. Mom and Dad are there now," Susan said in a more controlled voice.

"What! Why isn't he in Boston?"

"They didn't think he would survive the trip," Susan said and broke down into more uncontrollable sobbing.

Marty was stunned. The gravity of the situation hit her hard. Again, silence on the phone line as Susan got her sobbing under control.

"Susan," Marty said in a much more controlled and matter-of-fact voice. "Susan, I'm packing my bag right now and coming down to the Cape. You're at Mom and Dad's, right?

"Yes," a subdued Susan replied.

"I'll be there in about an hour, kid. Hang in there. I love you, Susan."

"I love you, too, Marty. Hurry, please."

And with that, the phone conversation was over, and the wheel of notification was set in motion.

Susan called our other two sisters, and the conversations varied only slightly. Nancy was the mother of six-month-old twins, and Judy was eight months pregnant with her first child. Neither was in a position to "drop everything" and come to the hospital, so plans were made to keep in touch about my condition.

After hanging up the phone with Susan, Marty called Gail right away.

"Hi, Gail. It's Marty."

"Marty, what's wrong?" Gail knew her partner well enough to hear the emotion in her voice.

"It's my brother. Susan called to let me know he was in a car accident and hurt pretty bad. He's in surgery now."

"Did Susan tell you why he's in surgery? How bad is he?" Gail wanted to know.

"Susan didn't know. My parents are at the hospital now. I'm going down to the Cape. I need to be there."

"Are you sure?"

"Yes, it's my baby brother, and I need to be there."

Gail knew that, when Marty had made up her mind, that was it—there would be no dissuading her.

"Alright, I'm going with you," Gail stated matter-of-factly.

"Oh, Gail—you don't have to; you haven't even met my family yet."

"Marty, I'm going with you. You shouldn't drive yourself. I'll pick you up in fifteen minutes."

This time it was Marty's turn to understand that Gail had also made up her mind and that there would be no changing it.

It was a quiet ride down to the Cape. Not only was my condition a great concern, but how the loving relationship they were in would be accepted—or not—by my family also weighed heavy on their minds.

Before Gail went to pick up Marty, she made one more phone call, to their mutual friend Kay. Gail wanted to let her know what was going on and where they would be if anyone needed to get hold of them. When Gail picked up Marty for the trip to the Cape, Kay was picking up her friend Joy. They were headed to the Cape as well. Both Joy and Kay were faith healers, and they were determined to come down and help me.

No one in my family had met Gail. We had only heard of her.

What a situation for Gail to thrust herself into: a bad car crash that, if it did not kill your partner's brother, it was almost sure to paralyze him, and the unknown of how she would be received by Marty's friends and relatives. Christmas had just ended, and the New Year's celebration was less than a week away. The demands of grad school weighed heavily on both Marty and Gail, and money was tight, especially this holiday season. It was a tough time, the kind of time that either binds people together or blows them apart.

My first full night in the hospital was December 28. Marty and Gail arrived at the hospital late in the day and decided to spend the night there, my condition being so bad they felt they should be close to me, in case I took a turn for the worse. This was actually more for Marty's sake than mine—she and I had not been close lately, and it now appeared that time had run out on any future plans to ever have a close brother-and-sister relationship again. Not that our relationship was bad, but we were both busy with our own lives, and rarely did our paths cross. Marty did not want to be far from her dying brother, and Gail arranged for her to spend the night, with blankets and pillows supplied by sympathetic nurses, in the waiting room just outside the ICU, where I lay in my bed, more dead than alive.

Before my accident, I was having a particularly hard time accepting that one of my sisters was gay. I didn't understand it. I felt it was wrong, and I was confused. I did know that I still loved my sister, but, at the time, I did not like her. Despite how I felt, Marty and Gail came to be with me, and their nonjudgmental friends showed up to not only support them but to help me. Joy and Kay found Cape Cod Hospital easily enough. When the front desk asked if they were family, they replied "yes." I already had four sisters. What difference would another two more make?

Joy and Kay went directly to the waiting area for the ICU, where they found a distraught Marty and Gail. They had been in to see me, and what they saw was worse than they'd anticipated. When they saw my un-moving body, the tubes going down my nose and throat taped to my swollen and bruised face, the gravity of the situation really sunk in. Multiple IVs in both arms, the plastic bottle taped to the side of my head, with one end going through my skull—it really drove home the point of just how serious my injuries were. When my family came to see me, their eyes could not help but be drawn to this awkward bottle with its bloody contents.

"Hi, Marty. Hi, Gail. I hope you don't mind, but we came down to be with you."

Weary eyes looked up at the familiar voice, and they were both shocked to see their friend Kay standing there with another woman.

"Kay—what are you doing here?" Marty asked.

"Marty, Gail, this is my friend Joy. We came here to be with you, and we think we can help your brother."

A little bit confused, Marty stood up and gave her friend a hug.

Joy, being the loving person she is, insisted on a hug from both of them, knowing the power of human contact.

"Where is he?" Kay wanted to know.

"He's just down the hall, through those doors right after the nurse's station," Gail answered.

Marty looked into her friend's eyes and asked, "Did I hear you right? You think you can help my brother?"

Without hesitation, Kay said, "That's right." Joy nodded in agreement.

"Oh, Kay—you are a dear friend. But he's really hurt; he can't even breathe on his own," Marty told her.

Without hesitating, Kay replied, "I know. That's why he needs us. You see, Marty, Joy and I are faith healers. We really can help."

"Really?" Gail asked, adding, "That's wonderful!"

Marty, her mind already on overload because of my condition, couldn't grasp what she had just heard. Sensing her confusion, Gail gently took Marty's hand and insisted she sit back down.

In a calm and reassuring voice, she said, "Marty, I've done a lot of reading up on faith healing. I think that it's fantastic and just what your brother needs."

All Marty could see in her mind was the bloody bottle taped to my head, my bruised face and tubes going everywhere connected to machines that kept me alive. *He needs a doctor, a hospital to heal him*, she thought. *Faith healing? I don't know.*

Sensing her doubt, Gail said, "Marty, why not? It can only help him."

"Okay, I trust you guys. It won't hurt him, right?" Marty asked, tears welling up in her eyes at the thought of her brother in any more pain.

"Of course, it won't," Joy said, speaking up for the first time.

"Don't worry, dear. We'll take excellent care of your brother."

There was something unique about her voice, calming and yet powerful at the same time. It made Marty think *Maybe this is worthwhile.*

Joy and Kay held hands as they passed through the swinging doors leading into the ICU and walked together to the nurse's station like they belonged there. The nurse seated behind the station looked up as she heard the two approach.

"This area is for family only," the nurse said, pointing to a sign stating as much on the wall behind her desk.

"We know," Kay replied pleasantly. "We're here to see our

brother, Jim Holmes."

The patient was new to the nurse. She had heard he had a lot of sisters, though, and these two looked harmless enough—rumor had it the kid was going to die, anyway.

"Room 216, third room down on the right," she said. "No more than thirty minutes."

Kay and Joy thanked the nurse and made their way to room 216.

Entering my room, they were pleased to see that they were the only ones there. The room was dimly lit, very still, and almost silent—except for the machines keeping me alive. *Perfect*, they thought, just the right environment they needed to do an effective faith healing. Standing across from each other on either side of my bed, they were anxious to start the session, before they were disturbed.

Both women placed their hands palm down on my body. Kay found a place free of tubes and monitors on my stomach. Joy had to move down to my left thigh. Once situated, Joy took the lead.

"Hi, Jim. My name is Joy, and I have with me my friend Kay."

"Hi, Jim," Kay said to me on cue.

"Jim, we are friends of your sister Marty," Joy went on. "We are here to help you with a faith healing. Don't worry—it won't hurt a bit. We are just going to put our hands on you, like we've already done."

She looked over at Kay and said, "Okay, let's get started."

They closed their eyes and breathed deeply several times, nice deep breaths, exhaling through the nose. At the same time, they were clearing their minds of all thoughts, except for one. There was no need for talking—the right state of mind was quickly reached by both women, and the all-important laying on of hands with the ailing patient had already been done.

The one thought in their mind they retained and intently focused on was that they were now deer, not any deer but a doe that had just given birth to an unresponsive fawn deep in the forest. Instinct kicks in for the "mother" deer; she knows that something is not right, and it is up to her to save her helpless baby.

Just as Joy and Kay were now deer, in their minds, I was now their fawn, and it was up to them to save me. Instinctively, the mother deer will begin to lick the fawn's body. This does two things: it clears away the embryonic fluid that may be clogging nose or mouth, and, most importantly, it is like a warm, gentle massage that will stimulate a non-working organ within the fawn to work as it should.

As a cold winter wind blew an occasional snowflake past the window of my hospital room, two women, literally strangers to me, licked my body with their minds in an effort to stimulate and revive whatever had ceased to work within me.

After twenty minutes of intense imagery, both women were physically exhausted and mentally drained. They had done all that they could do for now.

Before Joy and Kay left the hospital, they pulled Marty aside and told her that when they laid their hands on me, they got a strong feeling that, as she said, "Jim is in the process of deciding between life and death—all we can do now is let him know that his family and friends love and care about him."

~ Turning Point ~

Exact Date Unknown

My sister Nancy lived about twenty minutes away from Cape Cod Hospital, in the town of Yarmouth. This location was a convenient gathering place for family and friends. Marty and Gail had rented a hotel room in Hyannis, but would make the short drive to Nancy's every morning for breakfast. The rich and comforting smells of eggs, bacon, toast, and, of course, coffee filled Nancy's kitchen and the adjoining dining room. It was a good way to start what had become very tough days. It was comforting for them to be together, but my usually boisterous family was subdued, for obvious reasons.

With their daily routines nonexistent and worry for my welfare ever present, coffee had become a vital asset in keeping both Marty and Gail "up and running." Marty got up from the table to refill their mugs—she didn't bother to ask Gail if she needed one, too; she just knew that Gail did. As Marty reached for the coffee pot, Nancy's phone rang. Marty's hand froze, and she turned her head to look at Gail. This is what they had talked about—they should be ready for "the phone call." They had tried to prepare themselves and felt that they were ready to hear the sympathetic voice on the other end of the phone informing them that their brother had passed away. The phone rang again, insistent, impersonal. No one wanted to answer it, but Nancy had to—she didn't want the noise to wake up her six-month-old twins.

Nancy picked up the phone as Marty and Gail prepared themselves for the worst.

"Hello," Nancy spoke into the phone flatly.

It was, in fact, the hospital calling. "Nancy, this is Diane, your brother's nurse over here at Cape Cod Hospital. Nancy, I don't know how to tell you this …"

Oh, no, Nancy thought, *here it comes*, and she had to fight back the urge to throw up.

"Hello? Are you there?"

"Yes, I'm here. What is it, Diane?"

"It's your brother—he has made incredible progress in his recovery overnight!" Diane said excitedly.

"What? What did you say?" Nancy asked, incredulous.

Marty and Gail were watching Nancy, expecting her to burst

into tears. They couldn't yet tell by her reaction if what she had been told was bad news or good.

"Nancy, your brother is doing *so* much better this morning. We don't know why and can't explain it, but he is! He can breathe again, and all his vitals are looking better. He's still in a coma, but he's doing so much better. We all thought he was a goner. Oh, Nancy—we are so excited for him. It truly is a miracle!"

Stunned, Nancy hung up the phone. No "Goodbye," no "Thanks for calling." She just hung it up.

Gail asked, "Nancy, who was that, and what's wrong?"

Nancy wasn't even sure she had heard correctly; it couldn't be possible.

"Nancy, tell us," Marty prompted.

"That was the hospital," Nancy finally got out.

"Jim's nurse, Diane …" afraid to use the words she had heard, Nancy paused momentarily.

"Well?" Marty and Gail said in unison.

Not really believing it, Nancy said hesitantly, "She called it 'a miracle.' Jim's progress overnight—she called it 'a miracle.' They can't explain it … he's breathing on his own, and his vital signs are much better."

Now it was Marty and Gail's turn to be dumbstruck. Good news was the last thing that anyone expected when the phone rang.

"What? What do you mean 'a miracle'?" Marty insisted.

"Is he out of his coma?" Gail wanted to know.

"No, he's still in his coma, but he's doing so much better than anyone thought he would, all in one night!"

Before more questions could be asked, the shrill cry of a six-month-old baby brought everyone back to the moment.

"That's Dennis," Nancy said. "I've got to go get him up."

"Okay," Marty said. "Gail and I will do the dishes. Then we're going to the hospital."

Overnight a miraculous, unexplainable retreat from death's door. What happened? And why? It wasn't a result of something the doctors or hospital had done. No experimental drug had been injected into my veins. My Christian upbringing attributes my turnaround to an act of God, and faith. What else could it be? The faith healing? Possibly. It almost makes more sense than a straight-out miracle. Or maybe it was due to the same power I called on when I wanted my life to change, when I secretly hoped I'd be in a car accident. Was that power back and continuing to fulfill what I had asked for?

<p style="text-align:center">~~~~~~~~~~~~~~~~~~~~~~~~~~~~</p>

My sister Nancy's husband, Matt, was a prominent attorney on the Cape, with lots of connections and friends in all walks of life. He regularly called his contacts in the medical community to stay updated on my condition. On day thirteen of me being in a comatose state, Matt received a particularly disturbing report, even after all of my remarkable progress: A doctor told him to prepare Nancy for my impending death.

Uncharacteristically, Matt left work at noon that day, so he could get Nancy and bring her to visit me, possibly for the last time. I was now out of the intensive care unit, still comatose, in a private room. I had made progress with my breathing and the twitch of a muscle here and there, but it may have been too little, too late. Nancy and Matt entered my room to what had become, after thirteen days, the usual scene: monitors, tubes, IVs leading into a still and broken body. As Nancy and Matt stood by my bed talking to me and each other, they noticed my eyelids start to flicker, and then, incredibly, my eyes popped open.

I was back.

~ Scared to Be Alive ~

I remember opening my eyes—at first, being able to see again didn't make any sense to my brain. Everything was white and very confusing. I didn't know where I was or why I was there. As my eyes and brain came into focus, I recognized that I was in a bed covered by white bed linen. I followed the outline of my legs beneath the bed linen all the way down to my feet. Then a voice spoke to me.

"Jim, it's your sister Nancy. Matt and I are here to see you."

I recognized the voice, and I looked up from staring at my feet to the two fuzzy figures at the end of my bed. Slowly, my eyes brought them into focus. As they took on color, I knew who they were. I just wasn't sure.

Noticing my confusion, Nancy reached out and put her hand on my foot in an effort to comfort me. She repeated, soft and low,

"Jim, it's okay. I'm your sister Nancy, and I'm here to be with you."

I didn't understand at all. Why was I in a bed? What were Nancy and Matt doing here? And why were they looking at me that way? I tried to speak, but only squeaks came out.

For thirteen days I hadn't drunk any liquids, and I'd had tubes forced down my throat, so quite a number had been done on my larynx. I motioned for paper and something to write with. Once in my shaky hand, I was able to scribble out: *Where am I?*

Nancy told me I was in the hospital. I then scribbled out: *What day is it?* Odd question, in retrospect. When she told me that it was the middle of January, I took this information *very* hard. This loss of time was devastating.

My next scribbled question was simply: *Why?*

Nancy and Matt looked at each other and then back at me.

"Jim," Nancy started, "you have been in a car accident, and you are here to get better."

I was terrified. My mind could not comprehend what my eyes were seeing or my ears hearing.

All I knew was that something was wrong—really, really

wrong—and that it had to do with me.

That's all I remember about coming out of my coma. Exhausted and confused, I fell into a troubled sleep.

~~~~~~~~~~~~~~~~~~~~~~~~~

I knew that I was in the hospital and that I was broken. But I still did not really know why. I could only deal one thing at a time. The first thing I had to understand and accept was the fact that I had been in a car accident. Then I had to find out what was wrong with me. I had no idea and had to be told.

A doctor, I'm not even sure who it was, told me all that was wrong with me. It was terribly frightening. No one could tell me if my life would ever be normal again. They just didn't know. I was devastated to learn that my body and *brain* had been so badly damaged. Walking and talking normally again was all up in the air. It all depended on how well my brain recovered from its injuries.

As I digested the information the doctors were telling me, I just wanted to throw up and die. I did not know what to make of it— or myself, for that matter. As the reality of my situation sank in, depression gained a foothold in my existence. What had I done to
~~~~~~~~~~~~~~~~~~~~~~~~~

myself? What was the quality of my life going to be? Was it even worth living anymore? *I didn't want to live like this.* I felt lost, scared to be alive, *to be me.* I wanted the nightmare that was my life to just go away.

Several days dragged by, and I slept most of the time

Being awake had become a challenge. My mind did not want to acknowledge what my eyes saw: A hospital room full of machines and monitors all hooked up to me. As I slowly began to come to grips with my situation, depression grabbed more space in my mind with every waking moment. It was starting to cripple me, as only depression can.

But something mystical had happened to me when I was on life support, mired deep in a coma. The medical report states that I made a remarkable recovery, one that was medically unexplainable. A miracle? If so, how many miracles does one person get in a lifetime? And, again, why me?

In the four days I was conscious in the hospital, I shifted from deep depression to thinking, *Okay, this is the way things are. Let's get started on my recovery.* Nothing had changed physically; if anything, I was still learning about the extent of my injuries. No one had been in to talk to me about how well I would recover. That was impossible, as there were still too many unknowns. My future ability to walk and talk normally was still a big question, as was the extent of my peripheral vision, if I had any at all.

So, what happened to bring about this change, this second miracle? At first, I attributed it to God asserting his presence in my life, giving me the courage to accept my tremendous health challenges. This theory could also account for my unexplainable overnight recovery. In due time, the astonishing reason for my miracles would be revealed to me, but for the time being, all I knew was that I was no longer depressed. I now had a positive outlook. Even my sense of humor was back.

Don't get me wrong—I was still a physical and mental mess. But I was ready for the challenge. In fact, I could not wait to get started. Once I accepted my situation, my thoughts turned to getting back to a normal life as soon as possible. The change in my outlook was severe. I could barely think at this time, and I definitely did not possess the wherewithal to work myself out of my depression on my own. My attitude had to have been changed by something bigger than myself.

Though my change of attitude was not permanent, it brought me through the absolute worst of my depression in the hospital. The effect lingered for a while, but as new setbacks and challenges arose in my recovery, depression and despair would creep back in. This depression never lasted long, however. I always pressed on with my life and recovery, like some force was driving me. This positive outlook on life would prove to be the greatest asset in my recovery and in adjusting to my new life. But sometimes I wondered: Why wasn't I changed miraculously in one fell swoop? If God was going to bestow a miracle upon me, then why not fix everything all at once?

I was out of my coma but still in the hospital. I could not talk; my larynx had been crushed and dried out by life-support tubes. So I prayed. I promised God that if I could talk again, I wouldn't swear or take the Lord's name in vain. I was desperate. No one else could help me, so I turned to God, mediocre Christian that I was.

My voice is different now and not as strong, but if you did not know me before my accident, I sound normal. God answered my prayer, giving me a full voice again—but I have not kept up my end of the promise.

~~~~~~~~~~~~~~~~~~~

Four days after I came out of my coma, I was discharged from the hospital into my parents' care. It sounds crazy, but as it says in my medical report: "The patient made a remarkable recovery." I do not know if this comment applies to one particular instance or the overall recovery from my most critical injuries.

I was in the hospital for a grand total of seventeen days, thirteen of which I was in a coma. On day one, I had emergency brain surgery to stop the flow of pulverized liquefied brain matter coming out of my head, and, on day seventeen, I was released into my parents' care. I had recovered to a point where Dr. Weaver told my family, "There is nothing medically wrong with him that the hospital can help with. There is no reason for him to stay in the hospital any longer."

Unbelievably, no physical therapy or counseling of any sort was recommended for me when I left the hospital. I was released with only follow-up appointments with Dr. Weaver, to check on
~~~~~~~~~~~~~~~~~~~

my progress and healing. *My recovery was too remarkable.*

In fact, I was not at all recovered. I was a mental and physical mess. There may have been no medical reason to keep me in the hospital, but it was not reasonable for me to be released, either. It was great to be leaving the hospital, but I needed so much help—help that my parents were not capable of giving.

While trying to heal, my damaged brain could not effectively run my body as it once did. This is where my spirit—very strong from having been released in death—stepped in to fill the void. Imagine that your spirit, which knows it is supposed to live in heaven for eternity, now has a say on how you operate on this earth. It is a beautiful mismatch in so many ways.

But in my already weakened condition, things did not go well. Nor would they, for many years to come. To this day, I have no recollection of driving home the night of my accident, the car crash itself, or anything else over the next thirteen days while I was in a coma.

But I did start to recall where my spirit had been.

CHAPTER SIX

The Beginning of Recovery

~ Starting at Square One ~
Third Week of January 1981

*M*y eyes popped open. This time, I wasn't coming out of a coma; I was simply waking up. It was two o'clock in the morning, and my room was dark and silent, eerily illuminated by moonlight, just enough to make out objects in the room. It took a moment or two for my eyes to adjust before I recognized where I was. The built-in bookshelves, the multiple windows on three sides of the room, and the large door smack in the middle of the longest wall were all too familiar. I was in my father's old office, on the first floor of my parents' house.

My bedroom is upstairs, I thought. *What am I doing down here?*

Then the floodgates of my mind opened, and the stark reality of my situation gripped me like a fist clenched in anger. As I remembered my injuries, the car crash, and my death, a shiver ran down my body. I was overwhelmed and wanted no part of my new life. I didn't even want to think about it—it scared me too much.

Tick tock, tick tock. I could hear the hand-wound parlor clock in the kitchen several rooms away, slowly and methodically announcing the passage of time with every swing of the pendulum. It was a brief diversion from my troubling thoughts, a comforting sound on a cold and still January night. But nothing and nobody could help me anymore. All that could be done for me had been done. That's what the doctors told us. So, it must have been true.

I lay in my bed, staring off into the darkness, feeling desperate and alone. *My body is still so broken*, I thought, *and my brain does not work right.*

This is the best that all the doctors could do? This is as good as I'm going to get? I wondered to myself. *I am alive and out of the hospital, but my life is back to square one.*

Tears welled up in my eyes as it occurred to me that I may never leave this room, this bed. In the dark of night, my mind tallied up all of my injuries and the obstacles preventing me from having a normal life. I just wanted to cry, to sob uncontrollably, to let it all out. The first sob of self-pity brought about an unexpected result, and I had to stop before I even got started, as pain ripped down my right side. The muscles necessary to produce tears pushed and pulled on my fractured ribs, and the pain was so intense that it forced me to stop. My body denied me the simple act of crying—it seemed like I couldn't do anything anymore.

It is bad to be awake at night with your thoughts and physical pain. Everything seems worse with the light of day so far away. So I just stared up into the darkness, fighting hard to not have any thoughts at all. The few tears I shed would be dry by morning— tears that no one would ever know about. I was in this alone now. My parents would do what they could, but both of them were far from healthcare professionals. The bottom line seemed to be that my recovery was up to me—with maybe a little help from God.

No one had anticipated that I would be released from the hospital so quickly, and my parents had to scramble to make accommodations for me. They cleared an area on the first floor of their house, in a large room that used to be my father's office, when he first started his company. Into this space they put a rented "hospital" bed, where I would be spending a lot of time.

Like all patients being discharged, I was taken out of the hospital in a wheelchair, which was brought right up to the passenger door of my parents' station wagon. With help, I was able to transfer myself into the front seat for the ride home. I was weak and could barely stand up on my own without falling over. Once home, the car pulled up within a few feet of the side door. With help, I got out of the car and walked—if you could call it that. I used everything at my disposal to get me into the house: other people, the car, railings, the door jamb, and, once inside, furniture all propped me up and guided me to my "new" bed on the first floor. Once I got there, I was exhausted and just wanted to sleep.

<center>~~~~~~~~~~~~~~~~~~~~~~~~~~~~~~</center>

There are some very big voids in my memory during the first year or two of my recovery. Unless something poignant happened, one uneventful day melted into the next. It seemed impossible that I'd been released from the hospital just four days after coming out of a coma *and* that only my parents cared for me afterward.

My parents, with no training or guidance from anyone, used

common sense to try to get my life back on track. Mom figured that I needed a lot of protein in my diet to help my body heal. So, she would make me an "eggnog" drink every day, with raw eggs, milk, sugar, and cinnamon. I loved it and looked forward to it. She would also make liver and onions for dinner, which I did not like, but I ate it until I couldn't stand it anymore.

Dad's role in my recovery was to get me out of bed and moving again. The company my father owned was on Main Street in Falmouth, not too far from home, which was also on Main Street. So, at lunchtime every day, my father came home from work and helped get me out of bed.

My home recovery started with very basic accomplishments, which needed both physical effort and mental courage. First off, I didn't want to get out of bed. It had been my "safe haven" for weeks. I didn't know how I would react to being upright, and I didn't want to know. I was afraid to fail and discover all of the new limitations on my life.

At first, Dad got me out of bed and stood me up. Then I tried to stand on my own, without having to steady myself by touching something. For days, that is all we worked on.

Eventually, when I felt up to it, with his arm around me and my arm draped over his neck for support, we would walk around the room, *one time*. Then, exhausted and in pain, I would climb back into bed and sleep.

As I drank fluids and ate toast with butter and cinnamon sugar, made by my mother, my body eventually had to expel what I had consumed. The downstairs bathroom was just around the corner from the room, a total of maybe twelve steps away. But the distance wasn't the problem. The problem was getting there. The rented hospital bed could raise me up to a sitting position. That was easy. Then I had to lift and swing my legs out of bed. That was very hard. The muscles in my abdomen that performed this simple task wreaked havoc on my ribs. It would take several tries, each time inching my legs closer to the bed's edge, until I was finally sitting. Then, already in pain, I had to stand up. My father held my arm, saying, "It's okay, Jim—you can do this. I won't let you go."

My face white with pain, I didn't answer. I couldn't answer. I had to concentrate on standing on my own two feet. I didn't have the balance needed to do it. I wasn't ready. But I had to go to the bathroom. Dad put his arm around my waist in an effort to support me and, in so doing, pushed on my fractured ribs.

"Oh! No, Dad—you can't do that to me, not there," I said, wincing in pain.

Dad felt terrible to cause me pain, as he had already seen me suffer enough.

"I'm so sorry," he said. "What can I do to help? You tell me."

"Why don't you get on my other side and put your arm around the ribs that aren't broken?" I suggested, and that is how I made it into the bathroom.

Once on the toilet, my head spun, and I didn't feel I had the balance to stay seated without falling off. So, Dad would stay in the bathroom with me, his hand on my shoulder to steady me as I took care of business. My body was not "right" yet, and my bowels were no exception—what came out of me was bloody and sickening. It seemed like everything I did or tried to do was just an ugly reminder of the futility of my new life.

~ **Dreams or Memories?** ~

Sleep was a very important part of my recovery. Not that I could do much else. My body just needed to rest and heal. I had not been home more than a few days when I started to have some crazy dreams. But because I kept having them, they seemed like they were not simply dreams. They were so clear and real that they seemed more like something I had actually experienced. Because of all that had happened to me in the previous three weeks, my mind was reeling, and I could not understand or make sense of a lot of my life. My crazy dreams were always on my mind, and I started to ask my mother strange questions like, "Mom, did I sleep in Susan's room when I first got home from the hospital?"

"No, of course not. You needed to sleep in your hospital bed."

"Are the sheets on her bed white with green circles?"

I persisted.

"No. Why do you ask?"

"I don't know," I answered meekly. I was afraid of sounding like an idiot asking stupid questions about a dream.

I was confused by the seeming reality of my dreams, and I had so many questions about what I remembered of them.

When I slept, which was often, my strange dreams would come back, always the same. In my feeble way of understanding the issue, I assumed someone would know about my dreams and tell me what they meant. The dreams seemed just too real and important to keep to myself. I was sure a doctor would know about such things, because the dreams had begun while I was comatose in the hospital. After all, they were doctors, and they knew everything else about me. Doctors had become huge authority figures to me, especially since one of them had operated on my brain and saved my life. This was my reasoning at the time.

My mother mentioned my dreams to one of my doctors—I don't know which one—and he had no idea what any of it might mean. The general consensus between my parents and the doctor was that because of all the trauma to my brain and body, I was simply having some crazy dreams. "Just hear him out," they said. "Tomorrow they will be replaced by another crazy dream; no big deal."

The problem was that the "crazy dream" was the *same* dream, again and again, and, to me, it was not a dream but something I had actually experienced. The memories were so clear and fantastic that I needed some answers, and, in my crippled state of mind, I kept bugging my mother to explain them to me. *Finally,* my mother asked me to tell her everything I could remember about my dreams. And so, I did. In my slow and slurred speech, I told her all about the beauty of the summer day, lying in my sister's brass bed, and moving up into the flower to look down on myself and the sheets. How they smelled and looked. I told her everything I could remember about being in the galaxy of souls, surrounded by feelings of love. Revisiting where I had been was mentally exhausting.

When I was done, I turned to her with pleading eyes and said, "Mom, tell me what it *means*. Why do I keep having the same dream?" And then I started to ask her questions about what I had told her. I really needed to understand them. I needed an explanation of the dreams that were so significant to me. My mother was stunned and was at a loss for what to say. She knew that something out of the ordinary had happened to me, but just *what*, exactly, she didn't know.

One day soon after, Mom came into my room when I was reading in bed, propped up comfortably by pillows. She wanted to check on me and have a chat about how I was feeling. So, Mom pulled up a chair next to my bed, and we talked about lots of things. Eventually, the conversation got around to church. Mom casually mentioned that Robbie and I had been on the prayer list at the respective churches our families belonged to. These were the only two she was aware of, but there were probably more.

"Jim, honey, they have been saying special prayers for you and Robbie at church each week. The whole town is very concerned about you two." An innocent enough statement, but these words struck deep within me. They traveled beyond the basic recognition of my brain all the way to my spirit, and *bang!* Something clicked inside of me, and *I remembered receiving these prayers.*

More than receiving the prayers, I remembered *the faith and love contained in the prayers washing over me and healing me, both physically and mentally.*

But this happened while I was in a coma, I reminded myself. How could that be? The healing was like a warm glow that reached deep into the very cells that made up my body, healing where no scalpel or suture could ever reach. The memory was unbelievably mind-blowing, but I knew it to be true. Not only did I remember feeling this tremendous sensation, but it felt as if it had just happened. I was absolutely dumbstruck and at a loss for what to do or say. All that I could get out was, "Mom, I know. I could feel it."

"Feel what?"

"The prayers. I remember getting them."

Not sure of what I meant, she could only say, "Of course, you do. That's why prayers are said."

I didn't know how to respond. The realization was all too new to me as well. But I knew that this is what had happened to me. The "remarkable recovery," as noted in my medical report, could now be accounted for: *I had been healed by the faith and love of other people. I had been healed through prayer!*

Our family doctor sent one of his assistants, Dave, to come by and check up on me periodically. On one of Dave's visits, my mother mentioned my "crazy dreams" and my insistent questions on what they were about, mainly to keep him informed of all that was going on with me. Dave had been a medic in Vietnam, and had seen and experienced more life and death than any one person should have to. I liked Dave and really respected his opinion of my health. He was the first to suggest I may have had a death experience and that I was remembering my death in my dreams.

On that day, the dominos started to fall, and the dots began to connect. On one level, it all made sense, but on a hundred other levels, I was shocked, scared, confused, and everything in between. The crash, my injuries, my broken life, and now I had to cope with the reality that I had died and was remembering what happened in death? How much could I take? It may not sound like much—after all, I was alive—but, to me, it was just one more unbelievable thing I had to accept about myself. I didn't want to know anything more about this five-foot-eleven, one-hundred-and-thirty-pound finite being that is me. I couldn't handle any more. In a way, my "dulled" brain was an advantage to all that I had to take in. If I had been sharp, processing so much bad news in such a short period of time may have put me over the edge. Being in "low gear," my brain could only accept and understand limited amounts of information.

~ Homemade Physical Therapy ~

Without guidance, Dad continued to get me out of bed and "walk with me" every day. Slowly but surely, I could walk farther and with better balance. As I gained strength, it took less out of me. Eventually, Dad and I got to the point where my balance was good enough that I could walk without his arm around me. I was still unsteady on my feet, and I would stand behind Dad with my hands on his shoulders. Then Dad would say to me, "Okay, Jim. We are going to start off walking today, left foot first," and off we would go, shuffling around the room, left, right, left, right, one slow footstep at a time. As the days and weeks went by, we would venture farther and farther into other rooms on the first floor of the house.

A big day arrived when I felt confident enough in my walking and balancing ability to tackle the front stairway—actually it was just the first step. Several times Dad asked me if I wanted to try the bottom step, and I refused. Shuffling around the house behind my father was my new "comfort zone." I was not ready to leave it yet. I have no idea as to the time frame when this big day came. It must have been weeks, if not months, into my home convalescence. In this early part of my recovery, the passage of time was a blur. I had no idea what day of the week it was, or even what month we were in.

But I do remember that Dad and I shuffled over to the staircase, and I positioned myself facing the stairs. I reached out and touched the wooden banisters on both sides of the steps, the smooth and solid wood a reassuring presence. I gripped them tightly with my shaky hands. They were a comfort in my challenge to go up just one step. In my position facing the stairs, Dad's arm could not be around my waist for support, nor could I put my hands on his shoulders and follow him around the room one step at a time. *I had to do this on my own.*

"Okay, Jim. Pick up your right foot, and put it down on the step."

With the railings firmly in my grasp, I was able too get my foot onto the step. But was it in the right place? Was it to far forward or too far back? Would I lose my balance when I picked up my other foot? I would have to balance on one foot while the other was brought up to the step. I was already shaky on two feet, and I had to balance on one? I didn't know if I was capable of doing this.

"Now pick up your left foot, and step up onto the stair."

I was determined to do it. As frail and dysfunctional as my body and mind were, I had to keep moving forward in my recovery. I was driven to push myself to the limit of what I could do. On that day, the pathetic limit was one step up on a staircase, and back down. Just one step. *I had done it! I was standing on the step all by myself!*

Now I had to step back down. This proved more difficult than stepping up, where everything was in front of me. I had to step backwards and down all at the same time, and this was a huge challenge, to trust what I could not see. I was scared, as I didn't want to fall and possibly erase all of the forward progress I had made, never mind the possibility of hitting my head against the wall or floor. I was, after all, still missing a piece of my skull. There was only skin covering brain there, and it would not take much to put me back in the hospital, or worse. I knew that Dad was right there behind me. I could feel his hands on my back and hear his voice helping me with what to do.

"Great job getting up there, Jim. Whenever you're ready, let's step down."

I stood there, still facing the stairway. At the top of the stairs was a landing. If you took an immediate right, you would be in my sister Susan's bedroom—the bedroom where I'd had my death experience.

"Dad, I can't do it. I can't look down," I stammered.

"It's okay, Jim. You don't have to. Just do what I tell you, and you'll be fine," Dad reassured me.

"Okay. What should I do?"

"First, just look straight ahead; don't worry about looking down."

"Okay."

"Now pick up your left foot just as if you are going to take a step. Good, great," Dad encouraged as he watched me follow his instructions. Dad continued, "Now take that left foot and bring it back toward me. Great. Now lower your foot down until you feel the floor."

"I can't do it! I can't feel the floor. Don't let me fall!"

"You're fine, Jim. I won't let you fall," Dad reassured me.

I trusted my father, and, ever so slowly, I lowered my foot the final few centimeters, until my big toe could indeed feel the comforting hardness of the wood floor.

"I can feel it. I can feel it," I said as the rest of my left foot followed the lead of my big toe and made full contact with the floor.

"Okay. Now, let's get the right foot down," Dad said.

The right foot was much easier than the left had been, because I was not stepping back into an unknown void of trust. I was simply putting it down where my left foot was.

"I did it! I did it!" I exclaimed"

"You sure did," Dad added.

We went on to talk about how *we* did it, how I felt, and what we could do better next time. We were like two men analyzing a great sports play that we had seen on TV the night before. Then exhaustion caught up with me. I was worn out, both physically and mentally. I needed to get back in bed for a nap, and Dad had to get back to work.

After Dad left and I had taken my noontime medication to prevent seizures, I lay in my bed with the back adjusted slightly up, thinking, *This has been a great day. I'm really on my way back to a normal life.*

One step up, approximately eight inches, and back down … and that makes a great day? It really puts things in perspective.

Oddly, during my convalescence, I never forgot my name, birthday (February 10, 1957), and social security number, but I could not tell time. One sunny morning, I was sitting at the breakfast table, enjoying the warmth of the sun streaming through the large picture window, when my eyes were drawn to the antique parlor clock hanging on the wall, its consistent "tick tock" a familiar sound that had become comforting to me. The clock's case was made of wood, painted black; the face of the clock was white, and the hands adorning the face a contrasting black. At the very bottom of the clock case was a small square box with a door and glass window. Through the glass you could see the brass pendulum swing. The door allowed access to the pendulum for those times when someone forgot to wind the clock. Once the clock's key was inserted into the appropriate hole in the clock face and the spring re-wound, just a gentle push of the pendulum, and time was good to march on again.

I just stared. I could hear the clock tick, and I could see the passage of time that the moving hands represented, but what did it all mean? I could not decipher what time it was. The fact that roman numerals adorned the clock's face was inconsequential. Not only could I not tell time, I had absolutely no concept of the meaning of time. Time was irrelevant where I had been—dead. So maybe I lost the ability to keep track of time, because, in the grand scheme of things, time just doesn't matter.

Talking was also a challenge, both physically and mentally.

The physical problems I was dealing with that affected my speech—damaged and dried-out larynx and vocal cords—would heal in due time. But in regard to the mental process involved in talking, no one knew what to expect. My slurring of words was one thing, but it was the intense concentration I had to put into speaking that was most evident. It was a coordinated effort I had to go through in order to carry on the simplest of conversations. First, I really had to focus on what someone was saying to me, take it in, process what was said, form a response in my head, and then try to get it out in a coherent sentence. The simple act of talking to someone had become an arduous process.

Before I came out of my coma, my sister Susan had to go back to her job in Baltimore. I had improved greatly, but her vacation time had been used up, and she had to return. Ten days later, knowing that I was home from the hospital, she felt compelled to come see me and flew up for the weekend. She remembers that visit and later described my condition to me as "scary looking." She told me that I was very thin, with a long incision on my head that was held together by staples, and that a bone from my right, separated, shoulder was grotesquely sticking up beneath the skin. But I was alive. The last time she had seen me, I was making daily progress, but I was still in the intensive care unit. She needed to see me with her own eyes, to touch me, to see what no one thought possible. I could talk a little bit, so she would ask me a question, and I was slow to answer. She could tell that I had to think about what she had asked and then think about my response, which would be slow and slurred but understandable.

While visiting, Susan went to the bank where I kept my money and moved it in an effort to protect it from lawsuits. This was a prudent move. After all, I'd been the driver that night, and a lawsuit was a real possibility. As it turns out, there never was a lawsuit. Robbie's parents said that he and I were friends, and it could just as easily have been Robbie driving that night, and so it was not worth the effort and ensuing hard feelings. When Susan told me what she had done, I was grateful she was looking out for my better interests, but I will never forget the feeling of how utterly inconsequential money was. I did not care. Money had no meaning to me. Just like time, money was a useless commodity where I had been.

~ Mentally, Where Was I? ~

Having been released in death, my spirit soared to fantastic heights, all powered by love.

This innocent life-force then had to resume its secondary role inside my body, all the while not understanding why it was not unconditionally accepted and loved by everyone.

The more I had to interact with people in everyday life, the more my spirit shrank into the recesses of my being, where it could not be hurt by human ignorance.

While my brain was acclimating to life in this world again, my spirit was being proportionally shut out of the purity and beauty that dominated the other world where I had existed. I sadly realized that earthly life as I knew it would soon eclipse the world of love I had experienced. I will never forget that moment. I could look back into the beauty and light that is heaven while looking forward into the struggle and darkness that is this life. I remember this vividly, and *it made me so sad* to realize what I was leaving behind. But I had to move forward in this life. I had no choice.

My brain was having trouble functioning because of the damage to it, and now it had to process the retained knowledge of what it was like to die, be dead, and come back to life. The whole experience was very confusing. I couldn't integrate the two realities of spirit and mind. Like trying to mix oil and water, it wasn't going to happen. Each entity, this life and the beauty of death and heaven, had to stay separate, each serving its own purpose, hardly connected. The common denominator with oil and water is that they are both fluids but perform completely different tasks; while they may reside in the same container, it is impossible for them to ever mix.

But I could not separate the two existences in my mind for a long time. I had never heard of anyone having to exist with an awakened spirit in their consciousness. Not realizing that my spirit may be influencing my thought process, I didn't try to correct for it. You can't fix what you are not aware of.

Furthermore, I would attribute the dumb things that I would say or do over the years to brain damage, further prolonging my inability to recognize what was truly going on within me. I unknowingly tried to mix the two incompatible substances for decades, as my life spiraled downward, out of control.

Everyone told me I was lucky to be alive, and it was true. But, at the time, I was not sure, not sure at all.

I also realized I perceived life differently, seeing people in a different way. I remember one nurse in particular who took care of me when I was in the ICU. She was petite and very pretty, with golden blond hair. She took care of me when I was in a coma, talking to me as she checked on my vital signs, IVs, and all that.

When I came out of my coma, it seemed like she was always there. She was the only nurse I even vaguely remember from my stay in the hospital. And I was in love with her. An odd feeling for me to have, considering my physical and mental condition. Odder still, I also knew that she loved me. It obviously wasn't love in the normal context. My (at that time) strong spirit co-mingled with another spirit, the nurse's, giving my mind the perception of human affection. But that wasn't it at all. It was really love in its purest form, between two spirits.

Dr. Weaver, the neurosurgeon who'd operated on me, had his office in the same medical complex as Cape Cod Hospital. After checkups at his office, I would have my mother drive me over to the hospital so I could visit the ICU. This place and its staff had become special to me, as it was where I had come back to life. I always brought flowers for the staff because I felt so indebted to them. I appreciated all the ICU staff had done for me, but I really wanted to see the blond-haired nurse—I didn't even know her name—who I remembered so vividly. But my random visits seemed always to take place when she was off duty. I started to wonder if she really existed.

Finally, on one of my unannounced visits, she was there. I immediately recognized the voice, but not the person. She was not petite, had average looks, and her hair was a "dirty blond" color. This could not be her. What had happened? Where was that beautiful woman who took care of me, whom I loved and I knew loved me? What had happened was that my ability to see people for who and what they were, their essence, had left me. I had changed back to having an earthly perception of people.

I actually knew what was happening to me, and the realization that I was turning back into a normal human being, leaving all the beauty of heaven behind, was *very* saddening. I instinctively knew this was her, but she was nothing like what I remembered, at least not on the outside.

I asked her out on a date anyway. Despite not looking like what I remembered, I still knew I loved her. I had no idea what her age was or marital status—it never occurred to me to ask. As it turned out, she was happily married with several children. Of course, she politely refused. I accepted it on one level of understanding, but I did not really understand it on another.

I had, and continue to have, very poignant moments in my life, like God helping me when I turned my problems over to him when I was young, or when I saw the spiritual essence of my ICU nurse and the intensity of the love I felt for her, and the unexplainably good attitude that completely overwhelmed me as I lay broken and depressed in my hospital bed.

I had gone from existing in pure beauty as a spiritual being back to being human, from existing in a heavenly dimension to trying to fit back into our society. This was an incredibly hard and complex task, and I was totally unprepared for it. No one could help me, or even understand where I had been. I would stumble and fall repeatedly over the next thirty years, always picking myself back up, and blindly pushing forward toward what I did not know. All I knew was that I could not count on anyone to understand or help me. My success or failure was totally up to me—or so I thought.

I learned not to talk about my experience. No one could comprehend what I had to say about where I had been. More importantly, some of what I knew and wanted to talk about contradicted traditional religions. Despite my Christian upbringing, I came away from my death experience with some rather unorthodox views. And because I experienced it, I knew this newfound knowledge to be unquestionably true. Undoubtedly the most amazing quality that I came away with is the width and breadth of LOVE in our universe. It is the single most important element in all of creation. God is pure love—a caring and nurturing love. The universe of souls is full of the love we generate between ourselves on earth, and it has the ability not only to go with us in death but also stay with us for all of eternity! Death is pure love as well, albeit a peaceful, "all-is-well" type of love. *LOVE excludes no one.* I cannot emphasize this enough. It is one of the strongest certainties that I learned from my death experience. We all experience this love equally, both on this earth and in death, where we all belong and have our place—our home in the universe of souls.

If you believe that some people are not worthy of love, you don't fully grasp the meaning of love as I have experienced it. It is so much deeper than ourselves, our existence on earth, and the perceived good or bad that we may have done. It is beyond the normal parameters of our human existence, our interpretation of right and wrong. There is no score-card to be read or judgement handed down after we die, only love in abundance.

But, I thought, *who am I to talk about the way things really are? Do I know more about heaven than the well-established religions, just because I have been there?*

At the time, I clearly remember I felt that Jesus and I were one and the same. Not that I was the savior of mankind who died on the cross, but that I was pure of heart and mind. And, like Jesus, I had just left heaven. When I think of this feeling, I have a clear vision of seeing a man who looks like the Jesus as represented in church, and there I am—I can see myself in him. Jesus is clearly Jesus, and I am clearly me, but I cannot tell us apart.

When I came back to life, I was clearly different from the young man who'd died in a car crash on a cold December night, and this was a good thing. If I had died and not come back changed, it would prove that death was nothing but nonexistence for eternity. The only explanation I can come up with for my spiritually pure mind set is that I had been cleansed by being in heaven. This, to me, is just one example that heaven and a better existence after death do indeed exist. But this spiritually pure mindset started to erode the second I regained consciousness—that is just the way this world is. It had to be that way. The world we live in is material, and I needed my "street smarts" to survive in this—at times, brutal—dimension.

At some point into my recovery—maybe about a year into it—a young woman who attended the same church invited me to her house for dinner. I was sporadically attending church, as it was a chance to get out of the house and test my "sea legs" amongst friends. I gratefully accepted her invitation, looking forward to my first night out since my accident. This was a big undertaking for this woman; not only did she clean her house, shop for and prepare dinner, make arrangements for her two children to stay overnight with her parents, she also had to pick me up and bring me home again. I was petrified at the thought of driving again, and I lacked the brain-to-body coordination to operate an automobile safely, anyway.

Dinner was great. The mood was set, and it was just the two of us. After dinner we moved to the couch, but I couldn't even kiss her. Neither of us was married, the lights were low, and her cleavage inviting, but it all felt wrong, and I told her so. It felt wrong because, based on where I had been, physical love was such an abstract form of attraction. That is where my head was at. Logical in one dimension, and totally confused in another. I reasoned that God did not approve of the direction the rest of the night was potentially heading. So, I finished my drink—probably juice, as I was not drinking alcohol at the time—and asked for a ride home.

This night stands out in my mind because my decision to abstain from even kissing her was not a conscious choice I had to make. It was a natural decision that I didn't even have to think about. I just wasn't interested. Before my accident, I would have used this situation to get what I wanted, knowing full well this was not going to be a long-term relationship. A car accident would not have changed my twenty-four-year-old male mindset, but an encounter with God would have.

When I say, "an encounter with God," I mean that, in death, your spirit is totally immersed in God's love. This will cleanse you of all earthly thought and knowledge. You are the purest of beings.

My mind was reeling from all I had to take in—the accident, my injuries, my new life, and the memory of my spirit's journey into and out of death. But I wanted to do the right thing, always. I was scared not to. I liked the uncomplicated feeling of being pure. Being a good person was easy at the beginning of my recovery because I was not challenged by life's temptations. I was existing in the protective bubble of my recovery and was not yet fully engaged in all aspects of life.

As time went on and this world closed back in on me, the harder it became for me to remain pure, like I felt God wanted me to be. Slowly I slipped and fell from my heavenly state, ending up like I was before I died—just a normal human being.

I wanted to believe in God before my accident, but I was going on faith alone, and it did not always work for me. Then it had happened—I'd stepped into the afterlife that religion said would be there, and found it was all true. True and so much more.

Finding the words to adequately describe what I remember or sensed about my death experience is tremendously difficult. I have trouble defining what it is that I remember—it is like trying to explain an emotion or describe what the wind looks like. It is obvious that the wind is there, but it lacks the physical features to be adequately described. What really bothers me is that I cannot easily talk or write about an experience that is so real to me. The subject matter is just too overwhelming. Death, God, and love are very simple, but they play out in an astronomically huge dimension. Part of my problem in conveying this reality that I have experienced are the words available to me. They are too shallow to hold the exceptional meaning needed to portray where I have been. It's almost as if I should have my own set of words to describe the awe, the power, the purity of love that I have experienced. The words available to me not only lack depth but are also sometimes used in vile ways—they can be hurtful or demeaning toward other human beings. It's an injustice to use these same words to describe the beauty of death, the width and breadth of how each and every one of us is loved and cherished by God, or a higher being.

I don't think that our minds are equipped to understand heaven—mine certainly is not, and I have been there!

CHAPTER SEVEN

Grand Mal Seizures

*T*he key to a successful physical recovery is a black-and-white proposition: eat right, get plenty of sleep, do what the doctor tells you to do, and you will get better. I knew that I could follow this simple formula, and I was eager to get started. Little did I know that my recovery was about to veer out of the black-and-white and into more shades of gray than I ever knew existed. I still had no idea how badly damaged my brain was.

I was reading in my rented hospital bed when my lower lip went numb. I didn't think much of it; no big deal. Then my left arm and hand went numb, and I could no longer hold my book. The muscles in my left arm began to twitch, and I started to get alarmed. I had absolutely no idea about what was happening to me, so I called out for my mother, who was in the next room. She came to see what I wanted, and the only words that I could get out as my brain started to short-circuit were, "Left … arm … numb." And then all hell broke loose in my brain and body. I'd had a few seizures when I was unconscious, due to brain damage, but medication had kept me seizure free. Until now.

I had been killed in a violent car accident. Nothing could possibly be worse. Or could it? I was about to find out.

As my seizure kicked into full gear, my body convulsed, arms and legs jerking around as if I was a marionette under the control of a drunk puppeteer. My mother rushed to my bedside, but she had no idea what was happening and was just as scared as I was. She tried to control my flailing arms before I hurt myself or knocked something over. But my muscles were not being directed by a sound mind, and they had awkward strength, even in my weakened condition. Just when Mom thought she had me somewhat under control, my body went limp, and it was over.

My heart was racing, and I was gasping for air, more from pure fright than physical exertion. I tried to talk, but nothing came out. I could only flap my jaws like a fish out of water. Mom saw the fear in my eyes, and her first instinct was to calm me down and let me know that it had passed, whatever "it" was.

"Jimmy, Jimmy. It's okay, honey. You're alright now. It's over."

I got my breathing under control and was finally able to speak.

"Mom, what happened? What was that? Is it going to happen again?" I was asking my mother questions she could not answer.

"Mom, I was so scared, there was nothing I could do to make it stop. Call the doctor, please! I don't want it to happen again,"

I pleaded.

"I will. I just need you to relax right now. Would you like a cold compress for your forehead?" One of Mom's cures for everything was a cold cloth on your forehead, which did always relax me.

"I'll call Dr. Weaver's office in a few minutes, okay?"

When Mom called, Dr. Weaver was not available, as he was in surgery for the rest of the day. But the secretary said she would be sure to leave him a message.

What? I need help now! I thought to myself. I told Mom as much.

In her typical calming way, Mom said that we will just have to wait. She was sure the doctor would call as soon as he could.

"In the meantime, why don't you stay in bed and read? I'll get you a bowl of chocolate chip ice cream. That will make you feel better."

I had no choice. My rented hospital bed and the first floor of the house was my world. That's all that I knew during those days. After my ice cream, I read for a little while, until I dozed off, the whole episode having taken a lot out of me. I don't know how long I slept, but I was awakened by the ringing of the house phone. My mother answered. I couldn't hear what she was saying, but I knew from her "important" tone of voice that she was talking to Dr. Weaver. After a while, the conversation ended, and Mom walked into my room. She saw me looking at her with eager eyes, seeking an explanation, and so she just got right to it.

"Jim, that was Dr. Weaver on the phone. He said that you had a seizure and that you will be all right."

"A what? A seizure?" I asked, quickly adding, "Am I going to have another one? And when? Why did I have one today? What caused it? Oh, Mom, I couldn't stand to have another one. What did he say?" Again, more questions than my mother could answer, but I was feeling desperate and very afraid.

"Well, the doctor wants to see you on Thursday."

"Thursday!" I interrupted. "I need to see someone right now, not in two days."

"Yes, Jim, Thursday at two. Now, listen to me—he also wants you to increase your dosage of Dilantin and Phenobarbital He said that it will make you sleepy but that it should prevent another seizure."

"What do you mean, *should* prevent another seizure? Can I take more? Mom I don't think I can survive another one."

"No, we have to do what the doctor says if you want to get better. Now, here. I've brought you your additional pills and a glass of water. Why don't you take them right now?"

I had been taking medication since my accident. I didn't know what it was or what it was for. I just took it because the doctor told me to.

"Oh. Okay, Mom. Thanks," I said. I could not get the pills into my body fast enough. "I'm sorry to act like a baby, but it was terrifying. I didn't think it was going to stop."

"Well it's over now, and with this increase in your medication, you'll probably never have another one. Now get some rest."

"I'm sorry, Mom," I blurted out and started to cry.

Mom sat back down on the bed. "Sorry for what?"

"I'm sorry for all that I've put you and Dad through—the whole family, for that matter. I didn't mean to. It was an accident." And the tears rolled down my cheeks. I felt so guilty, a burden to my family. Couple that with my highly emotional state and the condition of my body, and I couldn't help it—I had to cry.

"There, there, Jimmy," my mother comforted. "We are family. We're in this together, and we will get through this together, no matter what." Then she kissed me on the forehead.

"Thanks, Mom. I needed that."

After Mom left, I put the cold cloth on my forehead and lay on my back with the bed sheets pulled up to my neck. I was too tired to read and drifted off to sleep, where I could find peace. At least for a few hours.

<hr>

I had suffered a devastating brain injury in my accident, but repairing the damage wasn't the end of it, like setting a broken leg or stitching up a bad cut. For the brain, delicate organ that it is, the physical repair is only the beginning.

When I asked why I was having seizures, this is the explanation the doctor gave me: The brain waves can no longer travel through the brain as they used to. A cut and the ensuing scar tissue are in the way. The brain waves then "bounce around" to where they should not be. The brain effectively "short-circuits" and, as a result, induces a seizure, which, in my case, involves the whole body.

Seizures range in intensity from auras—numbness or tingling in certain parts of the body—to a full-blown grand mal seizure, which is what I had.

On a scale of one to ten, with ten being the worst, grand mal seizures are a solid ten. This is not my interpretation; it is how the medical community rates them. Was this going to be my life, to be mentally alert while trapped in a convulsive body? I was the kid who could run miles at the drop of a hat, and now I was scared to leave my bed. I was petrified about having another seizure. I knew that I could not live a life that was dominated by seizures. *And I really wished that I had not lived.*

In the upcoming weeks and months, I would have several more grand mal seizures. The next one was when I was in the sitting room, down the hallway from my temporary bedroom. I was on the couch when I felt the aura coming on, starting in my lip, just like the first one. My father was there, and I told him I was in trouble. I'm sure I asked him to help me. Not only was I scared, but I didn't know what to do, and neither did Dad. Dad is a civil engineer, with no experience in what to do with a convulsing person. As my brain started to short-circuit and I began to convulse, one of my thumbs got caught in a belt loop on my pants. Very aware of what was happening, I started to panic. But my own body was out of my control. I was trapped in a convulsing prison made of my own flesh and bones. The seizure was bad enough, and now I had this crazy flapping arm beating against the side of my body. Probably the worst thing that can happen during a seizure is to constrict a limb that wants to convulse. It further confuses, in my case, a brain that was already dysfunctional. It felt like the energy that I would have expended in flailing an arm or leg, if held back, was then condensed and sent back into my body, which only made things worse. I could not call out or tell Dad what to do about my stuck thumb, as I could not speak. I could only watch helplessly as my body did what my damaged brain told it to do.

This seizure activity did not paint a pretty picture for my future. The more medication I took to control seizures, the less sharp my brain was. One of the medications I was on was jokingly referred to as the "dummy" drug, because too much of it made you stupid, as someone would later tell me. *Pick your poison.*

Not too long after my seizure in the sitting room, I had a seizure in the kitchen. My mother was there, and I said, "Mom, my lip—it's gone numb. I think I'm gonna have a seizure. What should I do?"

One thing Dr. Weaver told my Mother was that, if I felt a seizure coming on, I should lie down on the floor and put my wallet in my mouth, so I wouldn't bite my tongue off. Wallets are firm and soft at the same time and won't chip teeth.

Mom said, "Get down on the floor, and lie on your back!"

"Okay, okayyyy," I slurred out of my mouth as I got down on the floor, just as the seizure gripped my body. I had no wallet at the time, and neither did Mom. She grabbed a wooden salad spoon off the kitchen counter and shoved it in my mouth as my jaws repeatedly opened and snapped shut. I blacked out. When I came to, I was still on the floor, with the wooden spoon next to my head.

"Mom, it happened again. I hate these seizures! Will they ever stop?"

"Oh, Jimmy, I don't know. Nobody does. Dr. Weaver said that your brain has to adjust to the scar tissue in it, and then maybe, between that and your medication, you won't have them anymore. It could take years. We just don't know."

I didn't like the answer and remained quiet. I sat up and got to my knees. Mom helped me up as I grabbed onto the kitchen counter and was finally on my feet. Seizures leave you spent, somewhat confused, and tired. Mom took my arm and said,

"Come on, Jim. You need to get into bed."

She was right, and I didn't argue. I just wanted to sleep and wake up from this bad dream that had become my life.

Mom tucked me in and, as always, said "Sweet dreams" as she was leaving the room.

If only I could, Mom—if only.

Over a period of months, the frequency of my seizures diminished. This was a result of adjusting my medication, and maybe my brain was finally adjusting to its new makeup. In light of this, I started to take small steps toward getting my old life back. One sunny spring day, I was sick of being inside and needed something to do, so, I grabbed a broom and went outside to sweep the sidewalk in front of the house. The sanding trucks from the winter had left a lot of sand on the sidewalk. I took it upon myself to sweep this sand back into the street, so the town's street sweepers could clean it up. It was a simple task that I could accomplish and, more importantly, I was no more than twenty feet from the front door, so I could get back into the house if I felt a seizure coming on. That is how I thought those days; I was terrified of the next seizure, and I tried to plan accordingly, so I could hide my convulsing body, which I was ashamed of, from the public.

My mother was really worried about my ability to be outside. The whole time I was sweeping the sidewalk, Mom went from window to window, watching me in case I fell. Cars were going past the house, and many drivers recognized me and beeped their horns. I raised a weak hand in recognition, but I had to concentrate on just trying to appear normal.

The air that day was cool and fresh, and I breathed it in deeply, feeling the sun on my face. I was starting to feel alive again. I loved being outside. It was such a change from the sterile environment I had lived in over the past several months. I did not last long outside, however, as fatigue caught up with me after fifteen minutes of sweeping, and I had to go in and rest.

It was progress, though. I had gotten out of the house, done something productive, and made it back inside without falling down, or worse, having a seizure. I was recovering nicely, gaining strength and self-confidence, staying seizure free, and accomplishing small jobs in and around the house.

As the seizure-free weeks went by, I decided to join the sports center where Robbie and I used to play racquetball. It was within easy walking distance of my parents' house. Even so, it was a big step for me to leave the sanctuary my parents' home had become. The house was my safe place, where I could have seizures in private, and my thin and scarred body was accepted, not something that I had to feel ashamed of. I could not run yet to stay in shape—I tried, but I did not have the balance or strength. I was still missing a section of skull, and my better judgment told me to put off running for a while longer. I still felt the urge to do something athletic, because exercise had been an important and rewarding part of my life for so long.

Shortly after joining the sports center, I walked there mid-morning for my usual light workout. This was a good time for me to go; the place was virtually empty, and I did not have to answer well-meaning questions by other members about my health or how I got the long purple scar down the side of my head. I was embarrassed by my frailty and the scar and depression in my head where my skull should have been. I just wanted to work out, get some strength back in my muscles, and be left alone.

That day, I was using the universal weight machine, lifting pathetically light weights, when my lower lip went numb. I stopped lifting and waited for the numbness to go away. Then my left arm went numb. I dropped the weight bar and got up. I knew the signs that forewarned of a seizure all too well, and I knew that I was in trouble. I took a left out of the weight room and headed to the nearest exit of the building. I wanted to run outside and into the woods. I did not want people to see the frail, convulsing mess that was me. I wanted to run away from me and my dysfunctional body and brain. I wanted to run away from my life.

As I was passing the racquetball courts, the same ones where Robbie and I used to play, I knew I wasn't going to make it to the exit door. I was quickly losing the ability to control my body. I knew my muscles were about to answer to the whims of a dysfunctional brain. In a split second, I went from wanting to run into the woods and die alone to thinking, *Please help me, somebody, anybody.*

Just as my legs started to buckle, I took a step to my left, in the hope I would fall up against the glass wall of a racquetball court and alert the players inside that I needed help. I was able to get my convulsing body to bang against the glass wall hard enough to indeed get the players' attention. Then I blacked out. As luck would have it, the two players were a doctor and nurse who knew what to do to help a convulsing person. An ambulance was called, and I was brought to the hospital.

My mother had tried to talk me out of walking to the sports center that day. She had a feeling that I should stay home and rest. I, of course, would not hear of it. I wanted to lift weights, no matter how light. I needed to exercise and feel my muscles again. I needed to walk on the treadmill, no matter how slow, as that would put me on the track to running again. I needed that feeling of health and well-being that you get when you are exercising. This time, however, working-out put me back in the hospital, and I began to wonder if I would ever get my health back.

When the ambulance passed my parents' house with sirens blaring, my mother's heart sank. Instinctively, she knew that it was for me.

Fortunately, the racquetball court was on my left-hand side, so the left side of my body and head hit the glass wall. Had it been on my right side, things could have been really ugly. My ribs were newly healed, my shoulder still separated but healed, and I was missing a piece of skull on that side of my head.

This one was a particularly bad seizure. I spent the night in the hospital. The doctors adjusted my medication level once more, and, upon being released, I proceeded to crawl back into my protective "I'm never leaving the house again" shell.

I decided my life as I had known it was now officially over, and I wasn't going to try to get it back anymore. It was all over. I was done, content to live the rest of my life in my parents' house. I regressed mentally in my recovery. I was scared and fed up with my life—*screw it*. I wasn't asking my body and brain to do much, just a little exercise, which is supposed to be good for you, but my brain couldn't handle it. I was frightened about my future. What would it be like? Would I ever be close to leading a normal life again? Or would seizures keep me limited, unable to drive, get a job, or have any type of social life?

~~~~~~~~~~~~~~~~~~~~~~~~~~~~

At age twenty-four, I was thin and weak, with a body and brain that I could not trust to function correctly. With more surgeries on the horizon, it seemed like a long time, if ever, before I would be even close to normal again. Everyone kept telling me that I was lucky to be alive, but I seriously doubted it.

I did not leave the house for weeks. I was content to lie in my bed and read all day. Dad would come home for lunch, but I wouldn't get up. I didn't need his help anymore. I just chose to be in bed.

"You're going to get bedsores," my mother said to me one day.

"I don't care," I replied shortly.

"Jim, you've got to get up."

"No, I don't."
~~~~~~~~~~~~~~~~~~~~~~~~~~~~

"Jim, listen to me. You've got to get up and keep moving. Your whole life is in front of you."

"I don't care." Another intelligent reply from me.

"Well, you can't stay here much longer," Mom shot back.

"Whadya mean, 'I can't stay here'?" This got my attention.

"Your father and I have talked and decided you have to get back out on your own again."

"What? My shoulder is still broken, and I'm missing part of my head—and you're kicking me out? What kind of parents are you?" I asked indignantly.

"Jim, stop it. Of course, we're not kicking you out. But you can't stay here forever. You have to get well and get your life back."

"I can't! I can't do it. I'll have another seizure, and they'll put me in a home with a bunch of half-wits like me."

"Oh, no, they won't. Besides that, you won't have another seizure. You're only going to get better from here on out."

I hoped she was right, but I did not believe her for a second.

"How can you say that? How do you know? You're not a doctor. You've never had a seizure. I have, and I'm scared, really scared. Please don't let me have another one, please," I begged.

I'd had it with seizures and my broken body. But what could she do? What could I do? I couldn't go back and fix what was wrong. I could only move forward and hope for the best. At this low point, the "best" didn't look very good.

As the saying goes, it was "gut check" time. It probably hurt my mother as much to say it as it did for me to hear it. But she was right. I had to stop my crying, be nice to my mother, who was overwhelmed as well, and make the best of what was left of my life. Practically speaking, there really was no other choice.

That is what frustrated me the most. I had no choice but to "play the hand that I had been dealt." It wasn't the severity of my injuries—I knew they would heal over time. It was the unknown aspect of my recovery. No one knew what my future held, what type of life I would lead. It was the doubt, the not knowing, that ate away at my psyche. The only course of action prescribed by my doctors was "Let's wait and see what happens; let's see how well the brain heals."

I didn't want to hear that. I wanted the doctors to say, "If you do x, y, and z, you will heal nicely and be normal again." But they couldn't. They just did not know.

I just needed someone to tell me that everything would be alright, that I would be okay. I desperately needed to hear those words, even if they were a lie. I needed someone to lie to me. I needed hope, a light, no matter how dim, at the end of my recovery tunnel. I needed words of hope and healing that would never be spoken to me. This damaged me beyond measure, and for a long time to come.

Day after day, I lay in bed recovering, and I had a lot of time on my hands. I could read only so much, and I found TV boring. It was during these quiet times, when I was alone with my thoughts, that the damage was done. I couldn't help but contemplate the unknown status of my future. I feared that seizures would rule my body and that I would never lead anything close to a normal life again. This very plausible fear of my potential life gripped my insides and squeezed them until I was physically ill.

<div align="center">~~~~~~~~~~~~~~~~~~~~</div>

When I felt up to it one Sunday, I walked—with my parents'

help—across the Village Green to the Congregational Church to attend the morning service. At this time, I was still broken. My head was shaved, with shiny stainless-steel staples holding the long incision on the right side of my head closed. Before the service started, the minister looked down from his pulpit and welcomed me back to church. For the first time in my life, I heard applause in the Congregational Church. This was unheard of. And it was for me. I did not have the strength to stand up and acknowledge the ovation. All that I could do was smile and wave a weak hand.

As time went on and I adjusted to this life, I realized what fantastic news was contained in my death experience. I had this extremely enlightening message, with no idea of how to express it. I tentatively started to reach out to people who I thought would understand what I had been through spiritually. I really needed someone to understand and explain it all to me, as I was still confused and searching for answers.

After the church service one Sunday, I approached the minister and offered to tell him about my death experience. I thought that my story was so inspirational, so uplifting that church was the perfect setting for my story to be told. He then, in turn, could share the wonder and beauty of dying with the congregation. So, after the service that Sunday, I worked up my courage and offered to share my death experience with the minister.

He looked at me and, without hesitation or even consideration, replied, "No. I'm glad you're back Jim, but no, thanks."

I was shocked. Having experienced what he preaches about, I thought he should want to know all that I now knew. In my death, I had experienced the love of God. I felt like my church was turning its back on me, that I wasn't worthy of the minister's time. I walked away feeling like a fool for thinking that what I had experienced could help other people.

I had not attended church on a regular basis since I was young. But I did make it to the big three: Thanksgiving, Christmas, and Easter. Oddly enough, I counted on my church just being there for me—not necessarily going to it, but just knowing that it was there. The church had become one of the rocks in my life, never letting me down. I took great comfort in its unconditional acceptance of me.

If a man of the cloth did not want to hear of my experience, then who would? I was still in a fragile state, both mentally and physically. I started to doubt my story. Maybe it was just a stupid dream that my brain-damaged mind had conjured up. After all, who was I? I was just an average working stiff with no special credentials. Why would God bother to put his time and effort into me?

I really needed to talk to somebody about what had happened to me, about what I had been through, and the awareness I now possessed about dying and what it is like to be dead. It is such a basic subject, something that is going to happen to all of us, I was surprised that no one would listen to me, let alone understand what I was trying to share. I tried to bring it up to people close to me, but, as soon as I started to talk about God and heaven, their attention would wane, eyes would roll, and disbelief was plain to see on their face. I recognized it for what it was. I was making people uncomfortable by bringing up God and dying. I used to be that way, too, so I understood their reaction.

I also found that no one wanted to hear about my accident, especially in depth. Invariably, they want to talk about themselves or their own near-death experience. "If I had been in that car, I would have died," or "If I had been twenty feet to my right, I would have been killed." Or they knew of someone who had been in an accident that always seemed to be far worse than anything I had experienced. People brushed aside my injuries, as if they thought I was stretching the truth about them, as if there was no way they could be as bad as I told them they were. So, I stopped talking about it. I was struggling to fit back into life, which was hard enough, and it was easier to omit this part of my life résumé and keep it to myself.

<center>~~~~~~~~~~~~~~~~~~~~~~</center>

As time went by, my health gradually improved. I gained strength and was seizure-free for a while. My doctors felt it was time to install the protective plate in my head. I was excited at the prospect of finally having a "whole" head again. Plus, I had been told that my right shoulder would also be fixed. This was great news, as all I wanted was to put the accident and all my operations behind me and move ahead with my recovery and life.

I was also apprehensive, however, as installing the plate was major surgery and would expose the already-damaged part of my brain. I was afraid this surgery would disrupt the scar tissue in and around my brain and trigger more seizures. I was already paranoid about my health, and now I had something very real and potentially damaging to worry about. With my seizures finally under control, I did not want to go backwards in my recovery and have to deal with them again. But if I ever wanted anything close to a normal life, the plate had to go in, and the risk had to be taken.

Because of the size and location of the plate to be installed, Dr. Weaver had to use a pliable substance he could shape to the contour of the existing skull. Once the skin was peeled back and the area of missing skull exposed, he would mix together the components of this medical "putty." Due to the chemical makeup of this medical "putty," once it was mixed, Dr. Weaver had only a few minutes to apply and shape my new piece of skull before it hardened. He had to form my plate by taking into consideration my jaw, temple, ear, and the curvature of my skull. I have no recollection of this surgery at all, or any time I may have spent recovering in the hospital—it's just not there. But the surgery was a success, with no complications whatsoever.

The one memory I do have after this operation was when I asked someone, probably my mother, I'm not sure, how the operation on my shoulder had gone. I knew that the plate was in my head, and I easily accepted that. It was my right shoulder that concerned me the most, and so I asked about it as soon as I was able to.

"Mom, I know that my plate is in, but how did the operation on my shoulder go? It feels the same."

"They didn't operate on your shoulder, honey. It would have been too much for you."

"So, I have to come back and have another operation?" I asked.

"No, they feel that it will heal on its own and be just fine."

"But one of my bones isn't even in my rotator cuff anymore and sticks up. I look gross."

"The doctors said that if it causes you pain, they will operate."

I was getting mad at the doctors this time. "They said they were going to fix it!"

"Jim, listen to me," Mom said sternly. "They can't operate on both your head and shoulder at the same time. Who told you that they were going to?"

I didn't know who had told me that. Maybe I'd misunderstood or heard what I wanted to hear, not what was actually said. I do know that I talked to both the doctors and my parents about my shoulder and how much I was looking forward to getting it fixed. It finally dawned on me that they just placated me going into the operation. *Don't upset the dummy.* That's how I felt they all thought of me.

As my recovery progressed, I still had so many unanswered questions about my condition that paranoia set in. When would I have my next seizure? How would my broken shoulder work as time went on? The doctors lied about fixing my shoulder; what else weren't they telling me? My paranoia about all this started to build up and overwhelm me. I looked for problems, both physical and mental, that did not exist.

For example, I was paranoid about AIDS. I figured I must have gotten a blood transfusion during my operation, and I was *sure* I had received a transfusion of infected blood. This meant I was now doomed to die a slow and ugly death. I had survived my accident only to be infected by AIDS in the process. My imagination ran wild with the thought. I did not know for sure if I was indeed infected with anything, but my paranoia kept me awake at night. In the eighties, AIDS was new, not understood, and running rampant. Having convinced myself that I had it, I wrote a letter to Dr. Weaver and Cape Cod Hospital. I needed to know about my blood transfusion, who it came from and what I should do about it. This is how I came into possession of the medical records that I have attached in the appendix. Notice at the bottom of the operative letter, where Dr. Weaver circled the paragraph that says I received no blood transfusion at that time. No blood was needed? Head wounds bleed like hell, and my head was ripped open from the back of my right ear to about the middle of my forehead. I didn't get it. I should have bled like a stuck pig. It's possible that the freezing cold of that morning stemmed the flow of blood from my head. In any case, this lack of blood loss has always puzzled me.

It seemed like every day I was coming up with another problem I attributed to my accident and brain damage. Trying to figure out what was normal for me and what was a byproduct of the accident, I called Dr. Weaver. I told him I was having trouble buttoning the collar buttons on my dress shirt—was this because of my brain damage? He politely reassured me he had the same problem with the buttons on the collar of his shirt and that I was fine.

In my state of paranoia and mistrust, I noticed that my index fingers were crooked. On the next scheduled visit to Dr. Weaver, I showed him my fingers and asked if they had been broken in the accident, and, if so, why wasn't I told about it? This was the only time I ever heard him get stern with me. He told me I had not broken my fingers, or anything else that I did not already know about, for that matter. "You are fine, and it is time for you to get on with your life. All the damage that was going to happen to you is over. You will only get better from here on out."

As it turns out, he was right. I felt stupid for having asked the question. I was an imbecile sitting in front of a highly educated brain surgeon. I was wasting his time and intellect on crooked index fingers. He didn't say anything like that, of course, but that's how I felt.

Years later, I dropped by his office, just to see him and say thank you, again. He was pleased to see me, looked at my scar, felt the plate under my skin, looked me in the eye, and said, "I do pretty good work."

That was the last time I saw or spoke with the surgeon who helped give me my life back.

Through all of this, I was very confused about God. I was dead and should have remained that way. I believed God had allowed me to be brought back from death. I could have been in a wheelchair and blind, but, again, God had allowed me to be miraculously healed. Why? And why wasn't God helping me now? As a matter of fact, where was God? If God and I had the special connection I thought we had, why was this happening? If surviving was the act of a miracle, then why was I still so dysfunctional? I didn't think that miracles were selective in what they will do. But apparently, they are. Had I been saved for a life like this? Maybe God hadn't actually saved me, and I was being punished for things I had done in my life before the accident. There was so much I did not know or understand about what had happened to me, physically, mentally, and spiritually.

I was a mess and continued to slip in and out of depression over the prospects of my future. It seemed that the light at the end of my recovery tunnel for a normal life again was only getting dimmer and dimmer. Despite all the setbacks, I was driven to press on with my life—I'm not sure why. Any depression I experienced never lasted long, and I always came out of it ready to move in a positive direction. Having seizures terrified and depressed me. I hated them. I was tired of doctors and nurses and the smell of alcohol wipes. I just wanted the smell of pine needles mixed with ripe wild grapes on a hot summer's day and the sound of waves breaking on the beach as a refreshing breeze swept in off the cool waters of the Atlantic Ocean. I no longer wanted my old life back. I just wanted a normal life, a life without seizures and daily medication, a life where I did not know what it was like to die. I just wanted to be normal. But too much had happened to me. *Normal* would never be a part of my life again. As much as I had been through, the hardest time of my life was yet to come.

CHAPTER EIGHT

Who or What Was I?

~ My Inability to Cope ~

*D*umb, stupid, ignorant, clueless, spineless, and everything in between. Take your pick—they all applied to me. After the physical injuries were healed and the last staple and stitch removed from my body, the worst of my injuries took center stage. My mind, that place where I think, reason, and store intelligence, had been devastated by the physical injury to my brain. No amount of home therapy and meals of liver and onion could help me with this. I was in for the challenge of my young life, with no one to help me or even understand. I desperately needed my mind to be placed in an intensive care unit, to be focused on solely. I needed doctors and nurses to help my mind think normally again, just like they had done for my body to function. Unfortunately, it was not to be. There would be no "remarkable recovery overnight" for my mind, no unexplainable improvement beyond anyone's expectations. That well had apparently gone dry. This type of healing would be a slow and blind process, in which I would put one foot in front of the other each day, not sure if I was moving forward or backwards or side to side. I only knew that I was moving, and that seemed to be a good thing.

Still, I felt like road kill that had been eaten by a predatory bird and regurgitated into the mouths of its hungry young. I was raw and bloody and in no shape to take care of myself when I was thrown back into society and thrust back into the workforce. I was easy pickin's, and people would take advantage of my mental weakness for years to come.

<hr>

About a year after my accident, with my seizures under control, I was eager to face life on my own again. Brain damaged or not, I had to get back into society and make my way in the world. There was a driving force that kept me moving forward—*it may have been God, but I feel it was more likely stupidity*. I saw no reason why I shouldn't get back out there and do what I used to do.

The most basic elements to living on your own is getting a good job and being able to drive a car. As time went by and I gradually improved both mentally and physically, my neurologist cleared me to drive a car again. I had been seizure free for at least six months, which the state required. But I was petrified. I did not want to get behind the wheel of a car so soon. The accident and resulting injuries were still too fresh in my mind. But I knew that, in order to get back to any sort of a normal life, I would have to drive again, so I reluctantly started taking short drives around town in my father's pickup truck.

At first, I was not only scared about being in another accident, but my brain, hand, foot, and eye coordination was off. I jammed on the brakes too hard, accelerated too fast, and ran over a lot of curbs. My brain was on sensory overload, as the information was coming in way too fast as I drove down the road. My damaged brain had to process the information coming in and then, in turn, redirect this ever-changing information to my eyes, feet, and hands. It was overwhelming. Our brains are absolutely a fantastic organ. Sometime, when you are driving, think about all the calculations that are happening simultaneously in your brain. Distance, speed, angle of approach by other cars that are factored off of your moving vehicle as you merge safely into traffic, while at the same time, you are carrying on a conversation or listening to the radio—unbelievable!

I drove Dad's pickup truck because I felt safe in a larger vehicle. I have always felt that, if I had been in a more substantial vehicle than my Toyota Celica, I would not have been hurt so badly in the accident. There is no proof to this feeling, as the bottom line is that, if both Robbie and I had been wearing our seat belts, we wouldn't have been hurt so badly. Also, Dad's truck had an automatic transmission, so I didn't have to coordinate shifting. I did not turn on the radio or have any passengers with me. I needed total concentration to drive.

As my confidence grew in my driving ability, I would venture out of town on longer and longer drives. One day I decided to drive to my sister Nancy's house in Yarmouth, about thirty miles away. I always took the back roads, as I could not handle the speed of the highway yet. The final road leading up to her house was Weir Road, a long, narrow, and winding road that was actually quite a pretty drive through the woods. On this day, however, I could not appreciate the scenery. I was having trouble just staying on my side of the road while avoiding trees that seemed to be way too close to the road's edge on the passenger's side. On a blind curve, I unknowingly strayed too close to the middle of the road just as another pickup truck came around the corner. We hit driver-side mirrors in what was a very minor accident, but I panicked.

I had been in another accident! What would happen to me now? I did not want to talk to the police, my insurance company, or have to tell Dad. I hesitated—but did not stop. I drove away hoping the other driver did not care and that it would be over. After a couple of minutes, I figured I had avoided a confrontation with the other driver … until I noticed a pickup truck in my rearview mirror. Catching up to me, its headlights were flashing and horn beeping. As I pulled over to the side of the road, not really knowing what to expect, I got that sinking feeling in the pit of my stomach. The other driver jumped out of his truck yelling, "Hey, don't you know you're supposed to stop once you've been in an accident?"

I got out of my truck, my face still pale, my scar purple, and my hands shaking.

He came right up to me and said, "Didn't you know you hit me?"

I lied and said that I didn't. He knew I was lying because I had slowed down just after we hit, before I decided to take off. In an attempt to keep the police and insurance companies out of it, I reached for my wallet and, with a shaking hand, held out all the money I had. I said, "Here, take this — it should be more than enough to cover the damage to your mirror." I had no idea if it was or not; I just wanted him to go away. I wanted to go home, crawl in bed, and pull the covers over my head.

He looked at all the money and said, "What's wrong with you? What are you trying to hide?"

I don't remember what I said back to him, but he grabbed the money out of my hand, counted it, and laughed at the excessive amount. With a big smile on his face, he jumped back into his truck and drove away.

I was done driving. I did not need this type of confrontation in my life. So, I drove home cautiously, honked at by aggravated motorists the whole way, but I did not care. I just wanted to get home and never leave the house again.

Dad asked me about the crack in the mirror. I lied and told him I had tapped mirrors with another pickup truck and the other guy just kept on going. The chrome housing of the mirror had a slight dent in it. Dad never bothered to get it fixed, and, so, for years, every time I saw the dent, I was reminded of how I'd lied to Dad and how woefully inept I was driving that day.

~ Return to Work ~

I was extremely fortunate that my position as an estimator and job supervisor for Lawrence-Lynch, a local construction company, had been held for me. My employer was very generous, paying me every week while I was in a coma, as well as during my long recovery. The first thing I wanted to do when I felt up to it was go back to work. The owner of the company, Fred Lawrence, met me at the door my first day back. I will never forget the look of surprise on his face. He was one of the few people who visited me during my four conscious days in the hospital. He knew how bad off I had been.

"Jimmy, what are you doing here?"

"I'm here to go back to work, Mr. Lawrence."

"Jimmy, go home, rest, and take care of yourself. Don't worry, I'll hold your job for you."

"I'm fine," I insisted. "I just want to get back to work."

He hesitated and then said, "Okay, but take it easy, and let me know if there's anything I can do to help you."

Fred knew I had no business being there. I didn't.

No one told me I could not go back to work, I thought. That is how my mind was working. If someone had sat me down and said, "Look, you have survived a terrible car accident in which your brain was severely damaged. You need to build both your body and, most importantly, your mind back to a point where you can function normally," I would have protested. I thought my mind *was* normal again. Ideally this "someone" would have told me, "It's going to take years for your mind to get even close to normal." But this conversation never happened, and, sadly, I didn't know any better.

Like everyone else, my focus had been on the physical injuries. Once these healed, I thought I was good to go. But I slurred my words, especially when I was tired. And math, the most basic part of my job, was terribly hard. I was paranoid about making a mistake, so I would constantly check my work, adding and re-adding simple columns of numbers. Invariably I would make a mistake in my checking of the original work, and this would throw me into a tailspin of doubt and paranoia.

Telephones were the beginning of the end at this job. A conversation over the phone was very hard for me. It made communicating too abstract and impersonal. It really helped to see a person—to look into their eyes and at their facial expressions. Conversations over the phone with clients or vendors did not always go well, as the extra time my brain needed to process information would lead to delayed responses. I distinctly remember a conversation I had with a subcontractor as we tried to put a bid together for an upcoming job.

I don't remember the specifics of the job or even the type of service his company provided, but I do remember our short phone conversation. I was alone in the estimator's room, seated at my desk when the secretary, Peg, called me.

"Hi, Jimmy. This is Peg. Is Randy at his desk?" she asked.

I swung my chair to look over and saw his empty chair pushed away from his desk, which was, as usual, covered with plans and half-full mugs of coffee.

"Peg, no. He's not there."

"Do you know where he is?"

"Uh, no. I haven't seen him all day."

"Jimmy dear, I have Rick from Pavo Construction on the line, and he has some questions about the big bid that Randy is putting together for tomorrow. Do you know anything about it?"

"Uh, yes. I've been helping Randy with it." Randy had me doing menial tasks to help him, nothing too involved that could lose the company money if I made a mistake.

"Oh, good. I'll have him talk to you."

"Uh, no, Peg. Wait—"

Too late. Rick's voice boomed over the phone.

"Randy, Rick. I got your message. What do you mean I've got to be at thirty dollars a yard? You know I can't make any money at thirty."

Silence.

"Randy, talk to me."

I had finally found my voice. "This is Jim," I said meekly.

"What, who?" an aggravated Rick responded.

"Uh, my name is Jim. Randy's not here right now."

"Can you help me? I've got some questions about the Rt. 3

bid tomorrow."

"Uhh, I can try."

"I don't need you to try. I need some answers. Can you help me or not?" boomed Rick.

Silence.

"Hello. Hello. Is anybody there?"

Good question, I thought to myself.

Rick was a high-energy, hard-driving type of person who got frustrated quickly with my slow responses. Several times he barked, "Hello. Hello. Is anybody there?" He quickly concluded I was an idiot and asked to speak with someone else. I put him on hold and passed him on to Fred.

I hung up the phone and sat in my seat, dejected. I could not even carry on an intelligent conversation. I had gone back to work too soon and could not handle it or the social climate in the office. I lacked the ability to interact intelligently with my fellow workers, clients, and subcontractors, which used to be one of my strong points.

Not too long after this phone call, I noticed a new desk in the corner of the office that I shared with the other estimators. When

I asked about it, I was told, "Oh, yeah. We've hired someone to help you with your work." I thought that sounded odd, but I didn't question it any further. As it turned out, the new guy was not hired to help me—he was there to replace me. He was much older, with a degree in Civil Engineering and tons of construction experience.

Moreover, my old friends who I worked with did not treat me the same. I felt that they despised me for taking a paycheck I did not deserve. Eventually, I felt like I couldn't pull my weight and that I was an embarrassment to myself and the company I was working for.

I no longer belonged at the job I loved so much. I wasn't fired, but even I could see the writing on the wall. So, I quit. It was more like a "mercy killing." After all Fred had done for me— holding my job, paying me, welcoming me back—I just up and quit. It's a decision I will always regret. But I could not connect the dots. I was struggling to be normal, and I had lost too much strength, intelligence, and self-confidence. Above all, I had lost the respect of the guys I worked with. I could see it in their eyes. I was now a liability to the company, rather than an asset.

After I left Lawrence-Lynch, I got a job in town with another construction company. But it lasted only a few months, as I failed miserably.

There are huge gaps in my memory during this period, but somewhere in this time frame, I started seeing my longtime girlfriend Wendy again.

At the time of my accident, Wendy was working as an English teacher off the Cape, in a town just south of Boston. I'm not sure how she found out—one of my sisters may have called her—but she came right down to the hospital to be with me.

As everyone already knew and liked her, she was lovingly received by my family. She was even there when the faith healers, Joy and Kay, held a séance in a vacant meeting room in the hospital. All family and friends were encouraged to participate, Wendy being one of them. The séance was held not only to send positive and healing thoughts my way, but, more importantly, to try to "get through" to me, and maybe understand where I "was." Being comatose, I, of course, had no idea that she was there.

About six months into my recovery, Wendy rode her bicycle over to visit me at my parents' house. It was good to see her, but I knew that our relationship was over. I was in no shape to be with anyone, and I told her so. I was amazed by two things: One, how strongly I knew that she was wrong for me, and two, my strength to tell her. This ability to end a relationship so decisively was a trait I lacked prior to my accident. I just knew that it was the right thing to do.

I remember watching Wendy ride her bike out of the driveway, tears running down her cheeks. I felt bad about that, but good that I had done what I probably should have done years ago. It felt like a burden had been lifted from me. I needed to focus on my recovery, and I knew that being in a relationship was the last thing I was capable of.

What I did not know was that my mother also saw a crying girl riding her bike out of the driveway. Later that day, Mom came into my room and said she wanted to talk to me. She wanted to know what mean things I had said to Wendy to make her so upset.

"That poor girl rode her bike all the way across town to visit you, and she leaves in tears? What did you do? You know how much she loves you. What did you say?"

She then went on to tell me what a good person Wendy was and that I was wrong for making her cry. I had finally done what I knew was right, and now my mother was scolding me for doing so. This put me into a mental funk. I was having enough trouble with my damaged brain and seizures, and now I was letting down my mother and had reduced Wendy to tears. How could I do such a thing? *I must be a bad person*, I reasoned. Even though I felt so strongly that I was right about it, I must have been wrong in what I had done.

My mother told me, "Make things right with the poor girl."

Which, against my better judgement, I would do. It was only later that I realized how my mother had guilted me back into a relationship with Wendy. Any backbone I had gained because of my accident was quickly dissolved, and soon I was the malleable me of old. Before I was a year into recovery, I was in a relationship I felt I now *had* to be in, whether I was ready to be in one or not.

After several months, however, it just seemed natural that she and I were together again. And, crazy as it sounds, after a few years, we got married. It was on a beautiful summer day, in a picturesque chapel on Falmouth harbor. But it was only five years after my accident, and I had no business getting married. Maybe I was physically healed, but the mental part of my brain was still healing. I was far from being capable of making such monumental life decisions.

———————

At the time, I was working for a construction company in Rhode Island. I was hired to be an estimator, which is what my résumé said I could do. It was only a matter of months, however, maybe even weeks, before my boss realized I could not do the job I was hired to do, and he let me go.

With no job in Rhode Island, and Wendy not working, we had no reason to stay, so we moved back to Falmouth. I was good friends with my long-time family doctor, who owned a large house overlooking Vineyard Sound. There was a guest cottage on the property, and I made a deal with him to pay minimal rent and do landscaping on the property in exchange for letting us live in the cottage.

My memory is pretty sketchy about this time period, but I do recall when red flags started to pop up, warning me about my mental condition. One of my landscaping duties was to prune the privet hedge that lined both sides of the gravel driveway. The "Doc," as I called him, had electric hedge shears, power cords, and ladders in the shed. I was about halfway done with the hedges when I had to once again move the ladder. I was getting tired and grabbed the hedge trimmers by the wrong end while the blades were still moving, slicing off the tips of three fingers. I watched as my hand closed over the moving blades. My mind screamed *No!* but my hand did not get the message fast enough. Even the pain seemed to be delayed. Not the blood, though—it spurted out with every beat of my heart. Fortunately, the cuts didn't go clean through, and there was enough of a "hinge" left so the fingertips could be sewn back on. They would remain numb for years to come. My mind was still letting me down, this time with a delayed reaction to the obvious.

Once back in town, Wendy started going out with her old lifeguard friends, mostly on the holidays or weekends. I still really needed my sleep, so I didn't go along. Plus, it was her time to be away from me and with her friends. Sometimes she would stay out until two or three in the morning. I slept restlessly, waiting for my wife to return. I didn't mind her going out, but it did bother me that she stayed out so late. When she did come home, I would be awake and ask her questions about where she had been and who she was with. She would get defensive and say only that she had been out with friends, just drinking and talking. I could smell the booze, which was okay, but I really wanted to know what she had been up to. Something felt wrong. I felt betrayed. I told her so. But she told me that she was going to do whatever she wanted to, and I had to "put up with it." She broke my heart that summer, and the seeds of destruction for our marriage were firmly planted.

One summer day, Wendy and I were in the cottage arguing. About what I do not remember, but I started pleading to her for help. That I needed her sympathy and understanding, that I wasn't normal. She wanted nothing to do with it, and told me to "go get counseling," if I was that bad off. She was my wife, I said, and all I really wanted was a sympathetic ear, and some understanding, from someone who is supposed to love me.

I have never used my brain damage as an excuse or asked for help because of it. I was ashamed to be brain-damaged, and I felt inferior to everyone else. The fewer people who knew about it, the better. So, what happened next was terribly embarrassing.

It was summer, and the windows and front door of the cottage were open, letting in the cool ocean breeze. I was in the small bathroom, and Wendy was on the landing by the front door and stairs. Wendy went down the stairs, and I called after her, again saying that I had been through a terrible accident, was brain damaged, and really needed her help and understanding. I stepped out of the bathroom to follow her downstairs, and as I did so, I glanced out the open front door, into the driveway between our cottage and the main house. There, to my surprise, was the doctor's daughter and family unpacking their car for the weekend. All eyes and ears were directed toward me, the crazy man in the cottage. I was so ashamed. I had finally let out some very personal things to my wife, only to have it heard by people I didn't even know!

I needed to be accepted as normal, not looked at as a freak

missing part of his brain. I was devastated that my wife wouldn't listen and try to help me. On top of that, total strangers had heard my pathetic plea for help about my condition.

I was horrified. I felt like a loser. If my wife wouldn't stick up for me, who would? For self-preservation, I mentally curled up into my protective shell. Nobody was allowed in after that. Emotions and feelings don't go out. Simple, protected, safe. Since then, I have not asked for anyone's help or understanding with my damaged mind.

Despite our rocky relationship, Wendy was insistent on starting a family. It was a lifelong dream of hers. She also felt that her biological clock was running out. Eventually, she became pregnant and decided that our little seaside cottage was inappropriate to bring a newborn home to. Friends of hers had a summer home in North Falmouth, and they let us rent it for the winter. This is where we brought our firstborn child, Molly, home to.

With the summer season approaching, we had to make other living arrangements. I had an uncle who was a realtor in the neighboring town of Bourne. I borrowed some money and went out on a limb, buying a five-room house in the village of Monument Beach. This is the house that we would bring our first son, Rory, home to.

~~~~~~~~~~~~~~~~~~~~~

So now I was a husband and father of two. Even so, trying to fit back into a normal life proved to be an Herculean task for me in all aspects. I had to concentrate so much on the "here and now" that God took a back seat in my life. And yet, as much as I had no time for God, as I struggled to recover, God always had time for me—sometimes, in ways that I never could have imagined.

~ Pray for Adam ~
1987

Around the time Wendy and I had our first child, I got a job as a site superintendent for a local land development company, on the strength of my pre-accident résumé. My job was to be the onsite representative. I would oversee subcontractors during the land-clearing and road-construction phases of the subdivision,
~~~~~~~~~~~~~~~~~~~~~

a pretty simple job if you knew what you were doing. I had an office trailer onsite and a full set of construction plans and specifications to refer to if there were any questions from the subcontractors. I also had a boss above me to help if I could not answer a question, but his office was at headquarters, and he rarely came out to the construction site, as he shouldn't have to. I was provided with all the tools needed to do my job, and, if needed, he was just a phone call away.

For this job, the road-building contractor was run by two brothers. One was smart, low-key, and very good at his job. His brother, Adam, though, was a short-tempered, demanding man with a mean streak in him. The first few weeks of the project went well, as the work was simple and straightforward. Cut down the trees in the marked areas, remove and dispose of the stumps from the cut trees, strip and stockpile loam from the cleared areas on site for later use. Then the roadways had to be cut down or filled to subgrade, drainage and utilities installed according to the plans, all in anticipation of the final phase, paving of the new roads. After the trees had been cut and the roads brought to subgrade, the contractor started with the questions.

No set of plans is perfect, and that is why the site superintendent—in this case, me—earns his pay. When difficulties arise, a good superintendent can either get the answer from the plans and specs or draw on his work experience and common sense to answer the question and keep the project moving forward. So, when the first difficulty arose, it did not take long for this hot-headed contractor to see that I was out of my league and not right in the head. I had trouble reading plans and making sense of grade changes and slope equations, both of which I could easily do before my accident. The contractor was like a shark in the water that smelled blood. He attacked me daily, yelling at me, our faces only inches apart, his spit spraying my face as it flew out of his angry, profanity-filled mouth. His loud voice filled the confines of my small office trailer, growing louder as his frustration built from my reaction to him—really a lack of reaction, as I just stood there, stunned. My mind did not work fast enough to understand what was being said or why it was being said that way. I did not know what to make of this loud, hate-filled person who yelled at me.

In truth, I had no business being a site superintendent. The subcontractors looked to me for leadership, to keep the job moving, and everyone making money. When I mentally stumbled and fell, not only did I let down the subs, I let down my company as well. I was painfully aware of my shortcomings and did not know what to do about it. As I was now a family man, I desperately needed my job.

The attacks at work got worse. When I withstood the verbal abuse, and he failed to get a rise out of me, Adam threatened me with physical violence. It wasn't self-control on my part—some of it was fear of him, but mostly I didn't know what to do. Part of my psyche was made up of my innocent spirit, which had existed with God in the purest beauty of heaven. And now it was being exposed to an example of a brutal human being. My spirit looked to my human element to protect it from this merciless onslaught of vulgarity. I couldn't defend myself. I was too weak in both body and mind. Couple that with an underperforming brain, and I was no match for anybody. I was like a loyal dog that showed up at his master's feet every day only to get cruelly beaten to the ground and not understand why. I may not have been good at my job, but I did not deserve to get treated like this.

It was mid-summer, and the window air conditioner in my little office trailer was unable to keep up with the blazing sun that beat down unfettered on its metal roof. I was at my desk staying busy when I heard an all-too-familiar noise outside my trailer. A truck pulled up, the dark green 1980 Ford F150 that belonged to Adam. I knew the sound it made on the gravel as it jammed to a stop and the squeak of its fan belt that needed to be adjusted. As usual, he threw the automatic transmission into park before the truck came to a stop. Everything ground to a halt as the driver's door swung open with a loud groan.

I knew the sounds of his truck, not because I heard them almost every day, but because I feared them. Because I feared *him*.

Four fast footsteps on the gravel leading up to the trailer door and two quick clumps as his work boots climbed the two metal steps. I stood up. I'd made the mistake before of remaining seated when he came into my trailer. He would then lean over and yell down on me, and I was trapped until he was done. My pulse picked up, and, all of a sudden, my lips seemed very dry. Nervous beads of sweat trickled down from under my arms and ran over my rib cage all the way to the waist of my pants.

I watched and heard the doorknob being turned, and the door flung open.

"Jimmy!" he yelled before the door slammed shut.

"What?" I replied calmly, not wanting to stoke the fire of what I knew was coming.

He was hot—beads of sweat lined his upper lip, and his shirt was wet as well. His hair was disheveled, as always, and his brown eyes were wide and glaring as he made his way over to me.

"I'm trying to finish putting the catch basin in on Tobisset, and I think the layout is wrong."

"Why do you think that?" I asked innocently.

This set him off.

"Look, I've been building roads longer than you've been alive," he said, starting to spit sweat off his lip. He brought up his right index finger to point at my chest. "So, don't doubt me. I know what I'm doing," he said, his voice starting to rise.

"I'm not doubting you. I just want to know what's wrong."

He took a step closer to me, put his finger on my chest, cocked his head to the side and said in a half yell, "My brother and I are out there bustin' our asses tryin' to build a road in this damn heat, and you've got the nerve to question me?"

"I'm not questioning you. I'm trying to understand what's wrong."

"I'll tell you what's wrong—it's you! You sit in here with your air conditioning while we sweat in the hot sun. It's *you* that's wrong. What do you think of that?"

"I don't understand," I answered truthfully.

"Of course, you don't. You're an idiot!"

We were almost nose to nose. His words mixed with spit and sweat showered down on me.

"I'm not an idiot," I managed to get out. My face turned red, and anger rose within me, an emotion that was somehow awkward and strange to me.

"Why don't you hit me?" he taunted.

This caught me completely off guard. Me—*fight*? Violence? These were abilities I no longer possessed. I didn't even think about them.

"What's the matter? Just as I thought. You're a wussy," he stated as if it were a fact.

A lot of things were going through my mind all at once. *Fight, don't fight, he would hit my head, I'm not ready for that, I would lose my job if I hit him, what would my wife and daughter think, how would I pay the mortgage if I lost my job, and what was wrong with the catch basin on Tobisset Street?*

He stepped back from our nose-to-nose confrontation and his lips formed an evil smirk, showing his yellow teeth.

"What's between your legs?" he asked me, with a look of a superior animal that has taken down a weaker foe.

I had no idea what he was talking about. This time he yelled, "What's between your legs, moron? Pull down your pants, and let me see!"

Pull down my pants? What, why? I thought. Then the light slowly came on in my mind.

"C'mon, let me see." He was almost laughing now, knowing he had challenged my manhood and that I would take it.

The collaboration of mind and spirit that now ran my being had unwillingly uncovered a long dormant emotion—anger. This collaborative effort was now like a child with a new toy it wanted to play with, to test its limits.

I took a step toward Adam, postured for aggression, and I yelled at him at the top of my lungs. "Get out! Get outta my sight! Don't come back until we can talk like grown men. Get the hell out, now!"

Now, he was the one who was shocked. He scrambled out of the office trailer, and I kicked the door shut behind him. I was really mad. More than mad, I was murderous. I wanted to kill him, and if I'd had a gun, I would've shot him.

I slowly sat down at my desk and listened to his pickup truck pull away. I was shaking with a combination of anger, nerves, and fear. I really wanted to kill him, I realized, and that was not good.

But I'd had enough of his belittling me, of the constant put-downs, and the final straw of insulting me as a man. He knew what he was doing, too—he wanted to see just how far he could push me. Well, he'd done it. I was at my limit, and I seriously wanted to kill him. Worst of all, he would be back tomorrow. I may have won today's battle, but the war was far from over. Knowing the kind of person he was, this would make him angrier and more aggressive toward me, more demanding and more of a bully. The situation would only get worse, and it was because of me. What had I done? I needed my job for my family, but what little self-esteem I had was getting trampled. At the time, I thought there was only one solution to the situation: Adam needed to die. Obviously, that was not going to happen. So, I was trapped. I was at my wits' end with this situation and becoming desperate.

~~~~~~~~~~~~~~~~~~~~~~~~~

Lying in bed that night, I couldn't sleep. I knew I would get up and go to work in the morning, and so would Adam. Things could not go on as they had been. I could quit, but I'd had a tough-enough time staying employed, so I really couldn't afford to leave.

On a hot summer night, with all the windows open and only a sheet on the bed, I contemplated my future. And I was at a loss for what to do.

Pray. Pray for Adam, for his health and happiness.

What? Where did that come from?

It doesn't matter. I can't do it.

Pray for him.
~~~~~~~~~~~~~~~~~~~~~~~~~

The thought from nowhere persisted.

Then I remember the feeling I got when I turned my troubles over to God as a young man, the relief, the feeling that I would be helped.

But pray *for him? I can't do it. I want him dead and out of my life, and you think I'm going to waste my time* praying *for him?*

Yes, pray for Adam.

No dammit, not for him. He doesn't deserve to be prayed for, especially after the way he has treated me and made me feel about myself. Absolutely not.

Pray for Adam.

The thought persisted.

I had to reason things out. What were my options? Killing him wasn't really an option, so that was out. Quitting my job was an option, but one that I could not take, as I had responsibilities. Going back to work and putting up with Adam's abuse seemed to be the only option left for me to take.

What harm can it do to pray for Adam?

This question entered my head, but praying seemed useless to me. Adam was just too mean, a man I was sure hated me.

Pray for Adam.

This nagging voice would not go away, so I decided to give it a try, to pray for the man I detested.

I tried to pray for him, but it was really hard to do. It was like a physical block. It was more than that; I just did not want to pray for someone who had caused me so much anguish. *I'm not going to pray for someone I hate*, I told myself.

Pray for him.

This voice would not leave me alone.

I had to struggle to gather up the ability to pray for this man. It was not easy. I could see his angry face, hear his words that cut me, and feel the spit showering my face as he yelled every obscenity at me.

First, I said the Lord's Prayer, and then I prayed for Adam. Short and sweet, but I got it out.

Pray for Adam, again.

From out of nowhere.

And, so, I did. It was easier to pray for him this time, and it was a more heartfelt prayer from me.

Pray for Adam, again.

It got easier and easier for me to pray for this man, and, after several prayers, I felt at peace with him, no matter how he treated me from then on. I fell asleep that night praying for Adam.

Another hot day on the job site. Someone had tried to steal my air conditioner overnight, so I was busy trying to reinstall the damn thing when I heard Adam's truck pull up. *Something's different though*, I thought. The truck wasn't parked as aggressively as I was used to hearing, and his footsteps to the trailer weren't as quick. He came into the trailer, and I had my back to him, struggling to put the AC unit back in place. I said over my shoulder, "Morning, Adam."

He just said, "Hi, Jim."

"Hey, could you help me and hold this corner up while I screw it in?"

"Sure," he replied.

"Thanks."

"Hey, Jim—about yesterday."

"Oh, yeah. Adam, I'm sorry I yelled at you." And I really was.

"You were really pissed!" he said with a smile.

"You pushed my buttons," I said. "And besides that, it was hot!"

With the air conditioner back in place, Adam looked at me and extended his right hand.

When our eyes met, I could see the little boy in him. I felt the pain he'd endured that had made him into the type of man who could treat another human being as badly as he had treated me. I felt nothing but sympathy and understanding for this little boy who now stood in front of me, wearing the body of a full-grown man.

"No hard feelings?" he asked.

"No hard feelings," I answered.

And we shook hands.

"Now about that catch basin."

It was a miracle. Not only did my praying for Adam stop the verbal abuse, we gained respect for each other and developed a good working relationship. Adam and I would have our ups and downs for the rest of the project, but nothing like the confrontation we'd had on that hot day.

What could have brought about such a change? Prayer is the only answer I can come up with. The realization that prayer had made such a difference hit me like a ton of bricks. There was no other explanation.

After this incident with Adam, I started to understand the power of prayer in a completely different way. I slowly began connecting the dots of results—both good and bad—brought about by prayer throughout my life. The realization of how significant a force prayer could be was astounding. I still felt that I had brought my car accident upon myself in a misguided prayer to change my life. But the positive results of prayer far outweigh the unintentional negatives. My relationship with God and prayer was still up and down, but some parts of my sporadic faith started to crystallize. I finally understood that the love and faith in the prayers of other people manifested itself in the tremendous miracle of giving me my life back. This realization weighed heavily on me. I didn't know what to make of it or what do with it. So, I blocked it out and didn't speak of it for a long time.

The value of my church, the one I hated to go to when I was young, also started to take on a deeper meaning for me. I couldn't fail there. All that I had to do was show up and listen. It was a safe place, where people knew me and were genuinely concerned for my well-being. I would always get lots of handshakes and smiles. "Jim, it's great to see you. How are you feeling?" In an odd way, it felt like home. I had attended services here with my family, and, even though we hadn't been all together here for years, whenever I went, it felt like my family was with me.

I couldn't bring myself to attend church that often, though—maybe only a couple of times a year. It was just too hard for me, very emotional. I recall the minister preaching about the love of God one time, and I could barely stand to listen to it. Tears welled up in my eyes, and I wanted to fall to my knees and sob. I knew and had experienced just what he was talking about, and I was blown away. How did he know this? I had to die to completely understand what he was talking about.

Let me be clear about this: It was not the whole sermon, chapter and verse, that moved me, but rather an occasional phrase or paragraph of hope and love that struck a chord that did not exist in me before my time in heaven.

With tears in my eyes, I looked around at the congregation. They just sat there, unmoved. The minister may as well have been reciting a recipe for clam chowder. I wanted to jump up, point at the minister, and exclaim, "Don't you realize what he just said? Why aren't you moved to tears like me? Don't you get it?" But they didn't. They had heard the same words a thousand times, which now carried little meaning within them. But I had experienced the true and complete meaning of the words in death, and I was humbled by their depth and beauty.

Before the project with Adam was over, the company I worked for was bought by a much larger land developer, out of Brockton, Massachusetts. They kept me on because they had no one on the Cape to run things. It didn't take long for my new employers to realize I was "hanging by the skin of my teeth," and, shortly after that project's completion, I was told my services were no longer needed.

I was unemployed again. My wife did not work, and we had a second child on the way. I could barely make a living. No one would hire me. I had gone through all the local construction companies, and I had to go farther and farther away to find work as an estimator and superintendent. I continued to "bang my head against the wall," unable to realize I could no longer do that type of work, until I had exhausted all such jobs near me. Word had gotten out about me, and I was no longer being offered any work at all. Money became an issue, and no one was happy. I felt crushed by the responsibility toward my family, and I knew I needed help. But I had no idea who to talk to about helping me. Everyone, including doctors, all seemed to think I was doing fine—just that I wasn't very smart, and life was simply too much for me to handle.

In an effort to avoid the failure I was becoming, I started to drink. Drinking was not a solution to any of my problems, and I knew it, but it allowed me to keep my problems suppressed and out of the forefront of my mind. In the beginning, I drank at home, every night, after the kids had gone to bed. After a long day at home, Wendy was usually out with friends, so I would have only three or four Buds. I had to stay responsible in case one of the kids woke up. It was a bad road I was headed down, one that would only compound my mounting problems.

CHAPTER NINE

~ Rock Bottom ~

$\mathcal{S}$hut out from all construction work, I responded to an ad in the local paper for a job as a used-car salesman, at a dealership in town. I knew I had been good at sales and that people generally liked and trusted me. The job selling used cars was not an ideal profession for me, but I needed money and figured this would be a nice "filler" between jobs. I felt I was overqualified and would get the job easily. I called and made an appointment for my interview, telling the secretary I had no previous experience selling cars but was successful at selling construction work.

She said, "That's fine. We would love to talk to you, Mr. Holmes. Mr. Thorne, the sales manager, has an opening in his schedule this Thursday at 10 a.m."

"Great," I said, "I'll be there. Thank you."

Thursday morning, I showed up at the dealership at 9:45. I hate to be late. Before going in, I sat in my car in the parking lot for five minutes. It was a typical car dealership, mostly constructed of glass and metal. On either end of the showroom were two large doors big enough to drive the latest and most expensive cars through. I walked past the shiny cars on display and made my way to the desk of the office manager's secretary, conveniently located just outside his office door. I approached her desk, and, when she looked up, I introduced myself.

"Good morning, Ms. Thayer. My name is Jim Holmes, and I'm here for my ten o'clock interview with Mr. Thorne." I shook her hand and handed her my résumé.

"Thank you, Mr. Holmes. Why don't you take a seat in the waiting area, and I'll let Mr. Thorne know you're here." She got up from her desk and walked into the sales manager's office.

I'd showered and shaved that morning, put on wrinkle-free khaki pants, a blue and white striped shirt, casual loafers with socks, and topped it off with the staple of any man's wardrobe, the navy-blue blazer. I thought I looked quite good. From my seat in the waiting area, I could not see into Mr. Thorne's office, but I could hear every word said.

"Mr. Thorne?"

"Yes, yes Janet—what is it?"

"Your ten o'clock is here for the used-car salesman interview. I told you about it yesterday."

"What? Oh, yeah. Résumé," he demanded.

I could hear him flipping through the pages of my résumé.

"I wouldn't trust this guy to go down the street and buy me a cup of coffee!" he barked. "Get rid of him."

I couldn't believe what he said about me. There had to be some mistake. He was obviously reading someone else's résumé. I was honest, came from a well-known family in town, and he didn't even want to meet me?

I heard Ms. Thayer's footsteps approaching.

"Thanks for coming in, but the position has been filled," she said. She handed back my résumé, turned on her heel, and walked back to her desk. Just like that, I was dismissed from even getting an interview, lied to about the status of the job, and pretty much told to get out. I left with "my tail between my legs," defeated before I could even get started.

I knew I had been through a lot of jobs in the past few years, but, from my perspective, at least I was trying. Even though it had been years since my accident, I was still adjusting to the mental and physical tools I had to work with, and I was not really sure about what I was capable of doing. Self-doubt flooded my consciousness, made itself at home, and settled in for a long stay. Maybe I was useless, unemployable. I did not think I was, but the rejection without even an interview was crushing. I knew I had a problem, that my recent work history was not good, but, for some reason, I thought I would be "cut some slack" because of what I had been through. It was a miracle that I could walk, talk, and do any type of work at all—that must count for something, right? But, no. *What I had been through counted for nothing.* In fact, it had put me at a disadvantage when compared to "normal" people.

This realization of my unemployable situation was a startling blow I did not see coming. I was now not only discouraged but desperate. I needed somebody to give me a break. Then I remembered what my father's old business partner once said to him. When I was in the hospital, he'd told my father that, no matter what type of physical or mental condition I ended up in, there would always be a job for me at my father's old company. I always appreciated the gesture and kept it in the back of my mind as my employment "ace in the hole." As much as I did not want to, I now had to cash in this "employment chip." So, I went to ask my father's old business partner—a man I considered a friend— for the job he had promised would always be there for me.

Without calling ahead, I walked into the office building off the street, and asked the secretary if I could see Tom . Of course, she knew me and wanted to know how I was and how my parents were doing and all that.

"Shelly, it's great to see you, too, but is Tom available? I need to talk to him."

"Sure, Jimmy. What's it about?" she asked politely.

"I, uh…. I need a job," I replied.

She gave me an odd look. Then she picked up the phone and buzzed Tom's office.

"Tom, this is Shelly. Jimmy Holmes is here to see you when you have a minute."

She hung up the phone, looked at me, and said, "He'll be right out. Why don't you have a seat?"

I had worked in my father's company for about a year before I attended Wentworth Institute of Technology in Boston. I was always "the boss's kid" to the other employees, and I admit that sometimes I acted like it.

I heard Tom shuffling down the hallway. He was reading papers as he approached, his reading glasses halfway down his nose.

"Jimmy! Hi! How are you? How's your Dad? What can I do

for you?"

"Hi, Tom. I'm fine. Dad's good, too. Tom, I need a job," I blurted out.

I always made the mistake of thinking my accident and recovery had made as big an impact on everyone else as it had on me. Obviously, it hadn't and never would. Any promises made in the "heat of the moment" years ago had been long forgotten.

Tom looked me in the eye and said, "I have no job openings right now."

With that said, he turned and walked away, immediately engrossed in his paperwork again. Just like that, his promise of employment I had hung onto for years disappeared. I couldn't believe it. From the look in Tom's eyes, I knew there would never be a job there for me again.

My job "security blanket" had been ripped away. Once again, I was back to square one.

"Lying son of a bitch," I said to myself on my way out.

I was mad. And getting desperate for money.

This trend would continue, as I would try and fail at many jobs. I just could not get it together. At one job, they called me "Jimbo the Bimbo." I heard them call me this name and snicker. All I would do in return was smile sheepishly and walk away.

I beat myself up over my many shortcomings and all of the bad post-accident work experiences. The inability to do my old job at Lynch, other estimator jobs I'd failed at, the confrontations with Adam, the inability to even get an interview for a used-car salesman job, Tom's refusal, all piled onto my weakened mind and ego. Slowly I sank to the bottom rung on the ladder of jobs: I began mowing lawns.

Simple, easy, uncomplicated. Just show up on the same day every week, mow the same lawn, send out a bill to the homeowner at the end of the month. Easy, which is all that I could handle. Eventually, however, I was approached by a local family about buying their small landscaping company. I thought, *How hard can this be?* So, I borrowed money from a bank and bought the company. My employees liked me personally but wondered what was wrong with me when I said and did stupid things about the business that I really knew nothing about. It wasn't long before I lost their respect. The good employees left, and I hired almost anyone to get the work done. The quality of work went down, my good clients moved on, and my downward spiral of failure continued.

~~~~~~~~~~~~~~~~~~~~~~~~

For a couple of years, I made decent money doing landscaping spring, summer, and fall, but the winters always seemed to drag on, and any money saved was soon spent. In an effort to make up for this shortfall, I bought a boat, a sixteen-foot George Williams-built wooden skiff, for five hundred dollars. I then bought a 35hp outboard motor to put on it, for another five hundred. My plan was to go shell fishing—quahog, hard-shell clams—in the winter months, to make ends meet. As usual I was trying to save money, not spend it, so I did not bother to buy the two-hundred-dollar commercial shell-fishing license required by law. I was pretty much broke after buying the boat and motor, anyway.

Undaunted and determined to make some money, I borrowed a bull rake from a friend, so I could fish out of the boat. A bull rake
~~~~~~~~~~~~~~~~~~~~~~~~

consists of a twelve-foot-long aluminum rod with a "T" at one end—this is your handle, and at the other end is a wire basket about two feet across, with tines about one and a half inch long on the lower lip for "raking quahogs" out of the mud. As you pulled the rake across the bottom, the tines dug into the sea floor, and anything they dug up would end up in the metal basket— rocks, quahogs, fish, old bottles,you never knew what you might find.

Many a cold winter morning, I broke through "window pane" ice on my way out of Eel Harbor in Woods Hole, always taking a chance, hoping that just the right piece of ice would not open up my wooden boat like a sardine can and plunge me into frigid waters, filling my waders with water and pulling me to the bottom, a sure death. I always went fishing around Penzance Point, just across the sound from Martha's Vineyard. The bottom was terrible, full of rocks and not many quahogs, but because the fishing was so bad, the shell-fish warden rarely checked this area.

One winter's day, with the temperature right around zero, everything was frozen. I should have followed nature's cue and stayed in bed, lit a fire in the fireplace, and given it a go the next day. But money, or lack thereof, is a great motivator. So down to the dock in Woods Hole I went, stopping on my way at Dunkin' Donuts for a hot cup of coffee. Ice had formed overnight around the boat and dock. Even when untied, the lines used to tie the boat to the dock kept the frozen shape of the knot. Another good indicator that I just should wait for a better day.

A skiff is a wide-open boat, with no cabin or protection to shield you from the elements or provide warmth. I knew it would be brutal on the water that day, but the bills at home did not care about the weather and needed to be paid. The outboard did not want to start. I could tell that there was water in the fuel line, probably ice. This should have been a good indicator for me to go home and try fishing another day. But I was determined to make some money. So, I kept pulling the starter cord and priming the outboard until spark met fuel and I heard and smelled evidence of an engine trying to start. Finally, I got the outboard to sputter to life. I let it warm up and got my gear and coffee onboard. I untied the frozen lines from the cleats on the dock and gently steered the wooden skiff away from the dock, and off I went, breaking my way through the ice, out of the safe haven that

was the harbor, venturing into the open ocean for the short trip
to a favorite cove in Penzance. It was so cold, the wind didn't
even want to blow, and we glided, my skiff and I, into our cove
so I could continue my illegal shell fishing. I killed the outboard
and took in the silence and beauty of such a cold winter's day.
I picked up the bull rake, tossed it into the water, and began
scratching out a living.

Bull raking is tough work. They call it a bull rake because
you have to be strong as a bull to pick the damn thing up off
the ocean bottom full of mud, rock, and quahogs. The bull rake
handle gets as cold as an ice cube after a while, and, on this day,
ice formed on the shaft, as I pulled it out of the saltwater. I wore
insulated rubber gloves, but your hands still get really cold after
a while, so cold they ache, and doing the simplest task with your
fingers becomes a sick form of torture. They will just not work.
They do not even feel like they are part of your body. The ability
to unzip your pants so you can relieve yourself over the side of
the boat becomes impossible—your dexterity is gone. On bad
days, I would put my hands in my armpits to warm them up, so
they would work again. When really cold, the blood basically

leaves your fingertips, and without blood in them, your veins and capillaries actually shrink. When you warm your hands up again, the blood re-enters your capillaries. It is the worst, most intense pain I have ever experienced in my life, and it goes on and on, as it takes a while to get the blood back and flowing. Just when the pain is gone, you put your wet and cold gloves back on, grab the freezing cold shaft of the bull rake, and you do it all over again.

After a couple of hours on that cold morning, I'd had enough. The sun was not out yet, and the temperature would not be going up that day. My body temperature was going down because I'd put my freezing hands in my armpits so many times. The fishing was lousy, and I could not take the pain in my hands anymore. I pulled the anchor, eagerly wanting to leave the cold and agony behind. I could already taste the hot coffee I'd get at Dunkin's on my way home. Having stowed the anchor and the rest of my fishing gear, I gave the starter cord a pull. Nothing, not even a sputter. I pulled again, nothing. I checked the fuel, made sure it was getting to the outboard, and pulled the starter cord again. Nothing.

This was not funny. I could see houses on Penzance, but

they were all million-dollar summer mansions, and I was in a secluded cove—no one would see me even if it was summer. I had no cell phone at the time, and even if I had, I knew no one with a boat in the water in the middle of winter. Calling the Coast Guard would have been out of the question. The fine for illegal shell fishing and the fines I would have gotten for the safety violations on my boat probably would have landed me in jail. So, I was on my own, and I had two choices: fix the outboard or die from hypothermia.

I threw the anchor back overboard, as I was starting to drift out to sea on the outgoing tide. I could not swim to shore. Leaving the boat meant certain death. My only choice was to get the outboard running. I pulled and pulled the starter cord. Nothing. I checked the fuel again, spark plug, air filter, any and everything. All looked fine. As time went on, I started to feel desperate. At least the sun was coming out. I reasoned that, on the trip over to Penzance that morning, water must have been sucked from the fuel tank along with fuel. That water was now in the carburetor and probably frozen. I pulled the cover off the outboard and let the winter sun shine directly on the iced-up carburetor. I didn't have the tools on board to remove the carburetor and clean out the ice. Even if I did, when you drop a tool or vital part of your motor in the water, it goes to the bottom. You can't just reach down and pick it up; eight feet of water might as well be eighty. I would have gone from being screwed to being royally screwed if I had dropped something. Hoping that the winter sun would be strong enough to dislodge some of the ice in the carburetor was not only a long shot—it was my only one.

I told no one, including my wife, exactly where I went fishing. In my opinion, the fewer people who knew about where I conducted my illegal activities, the better. The only problem with this train of thought is that no one knew where to look for me if I went missing. Wendy did know the general vicinity, Woods Hole, but the cove I had chosen was well hidden. It would take a long time for search teams to find me, even in daylight. If I didn't show up at home, Wendy would figure that I had just stopped at a bar somewhere for a few beers, nothing out of the ordinary. By the time she called the Coast Guard, it would have been dark and late. My chances of survival would be very low. The sun got higher in the sky, and I hoped it would free up just a trickle of gas to get the outboard going. I lay huddled on the floorboards, conserving strength and trying to absorb some of the sun's warmth for myself. I was desperate, starting to freeze, and I didn't know what else to do. I was really going to miss my kids, and I felt really bad about being such a loser of a father. Fair-weather Christian that I was, it finally dawned on me to pray. It wasn't a pretty prayer—rather one laced with obscenities because I was mad at my circumstances in life, and I was mad at God. "I was dead. Why didn't you just leave me there? I was happy and warm. What the hell, God? All right, I'm sorry for all the things that I have done wrong. Are you happy now? Speak to me! I know you're listening, probably laughing at me, like everybody else. Yeah, well, you can screw, too. I don't care."

Then my kids popped into my head and I did care.

I may be well on my way to being a frozen Christian, I thought, *but I'm not going down without a fight*. I primed the outboard, got a firm grip on the rubber handle of the pull cord, and gave it a pull in anger. The damn thing broke!

"Really, God? This is what I get for praying? I thought it was supposed to help!"

Okay, I thought, *just calm down. This is an easy fix: Think of your kids.*

I wound the longer end of the broken cord around the top of the motor. *Pull gently*, I told myself, *gently. Don't make a bad situation worse.* On the second pull, the engine sputtered, wanting to run but still not getting enough fuel. I prayed again. No swearing, though. "Okay, brother—this is it. Help me out." That's how I pray sometimes.

I pulled the starter cord again, expecting the same result, only this time the outboard roared to life, sputtering as the last of the water went through the system, and then she purred. I pulled the anchor and hastily threw it into the bow, gunned the engine and headed for the safety of Eel Pond Harbor. *This was it*, my only chance to get home that day. I bounced across the now choppy water, going as fast as I could, with tears on my cheeks as the harsh winter wind combined with saltwater spray assaulted my naked eyes. Ice had refrozen in the channel since I had left that morning. *Screw the ice, screw this wooden boat, I don't give a damn, I need a drink.* All that I cared about right then was getting into my truck and turning on the heat. If the damn boat sank at the dock overnight, it would be doing me a favor.

I made it back to the dock, threw my gear into my truck, and started the engine. It took a while, but the heat finally came through into the cab. I put my hands on the dashboard vents, and the blood started to return to my fingertips, and with the returning blood came the pain.

As bad as that day had been, I would be back tomorrow. I would break the ice with my wooden boat, curse the cold, and be brought to tears once again by the pain in my hands. I did what I had to do.

God answered my prayers that day in a way that was best for me to continue developing as a person. *Help at arm's length*—no divine rescue from out of nowhere. I had to do my part as well.

~ Tommy ~

1996

At the time of my accident, my sister Judy was eight months pregnant with her first child. Upon receiving the news, she and her husband left their home in Swansea, Massachusetts, and drove directly to Cape Cod Hospital. When Judy saw me lying comatose in the intensive care unit, she was overwhelmed and broke down crying uncontrollably. Judy and I had always been close growing up. Being the youngest children in the family, we'd played around the house together and had spent a lot of time playing games in the back seat of my parents' car on our frequent trips to Maine.

The concern of my family shifted to Judy's health and the well-being of her unborn baby. She was encouraged to go home and take care of herself. Four weeks later, she gave birth to a healthy baby boy, Tommy. Judy did not see me again, understandably, until late February or early March. I was home resting in my rented hospital bed when she came to see me. As she would describe to me years later, I was there physically, but I had trouble talking and could not carry on a conversation. I was not really with it, not fully engaged in life.

Judy and her husband, Barry, had just built a house in Swansea to accommodate their anticipated growing family. Several years later, Judy would give birth to their second child, Jillian. Like my mother, Judy would play the piano in her house when she was happy. As she once told me, she wasn't a great piano player, but she loved to play, and Tommy and Jillian really enjoyed it. Barry had a job teaching math in high school, and he coached the football team. Both of their children were happy and healthy. Judy was fulfilled being a mother and housewife. Singing and playing the piano was a pure expression of joy with her life.

Tommy died in a car accident at the age of sixteen. He was a great kid, the kind of person everybody couldn't help but like. He was big, strong, and loved to play football. It seemed that with Tommy's size, strength, and agility, at least some level of college football was in his future. He dreamed of playing for Notre Dame.

The accident happened in the middle of a sunny summer day. He was in the back seat of a small SUV, and an inexperienced sixteen-year-old was behind the wheel. Tommy's father had warned him not to ride with his friends when they first got their driver's license. Let them get some experience. Too much could go wrong.

They were on a back road, and a slight drift into oncoming traffic coupled with a quick overreaction back into his lane flipped the SUV. Tommy, like me, was not wearing his seatbelt and he suffered massive head injuries, not unlike mine. He also went into a comatose state, just like I had. Word spread quickly throughout my family, and, just as they all had done for me, we all converged at the hospital to support each other. As I stepped out of the elevator and started to make my way toward Tommy's room, I saw my sister and brother-in-law seated on a couch. They were speaking with a doctor, just like the conversation my parents had with Dr. Weaver about my condition sixteen years earlier. This conversation went about the same: "Severe brain injury, not breathing on his own, probably will not survive." Like my parents, that is all they heard.

Judy sobbed as her heart broke, and her mind went into denial. She did not want to talk to anyone or be held. She wanted to un-hear what she had just heard and make this all go away. If she did not know about it, it did not happen, and Tommy would be home when she got there, probably watching baseball on TV and wondering what was for dinner. Then she heard the sounds of a hospital, saw her teary-eyed family, and the reality of the situation came crashing back to her, that her Tommy was badly hurt and in the hospital. She cried so hard that her thin body shook, and she wailed because of the unbearable pain she felt inside. My brother-in-law looked up and saw me walking toward them. When I got close enough, he pointed at me and said to the doctor, "Tommy can survive this—here's living proof," meaning me and my miracle recovery from similar injuries. I will never forget the look of desperation in Barry's eyes. He was grasping for hope, for anything but what the doctor had just told them. The doctor turned and took one look at me and how good I looked sixteen years after my accident and said, "No, it's not possible. Tommy's injuries are much worse than his could ever have been."

Like most people, without knowing anything about me or my accident, the doctor totally dismissed what I had been through. I know it was not about me this time, and that even if the doctor knew about my medical history, it would not help the current tragic situation. But it drove home that while I looked good on the outside, inside, I was still a mess and very confused about why my life had been spared.

Two massive head injuries in car accidents to two young

men in the same family in a span of sixteen years. Both of us would have to fight to survive while in a coma, as our families dealt with their own heartache and pain. The two accidents and resulting injuries were too similar. Because I had survived, it gave us all hope, and we expected another miracle. Tragically, this time, it was not to be.

Eventually, my sister and brother-in-law had to concede hope and let their son be taken off life support. Unlike me, his brain could not recover from the damage done to it. Judy was in Tommy's room when he was taken off life support. Through her tears she could see the pulse of her son's heart in a vein in his neck—slowly it got more difficult for her to see the only sign of life in her son, until the pulsing stopped, never to return. Tommy was dead.

As my sister looked at her son, she felt someone leaning up against her back, like they were trying to get a better view over her shoulder. She turned to see who it was, and, to her surprise, no one was there. Either God was there to support her, or Tommy had hugged her on his way out of the room. No one will ever know which it was, but she clearly recalls the feeling of someone up against her at this terrible moment in her life. Tommy lives on in his family, a lovable young man with a great sense of humor and a passion for sports. He also lives on in strangers, people who we will never meet, people who owe their lives to Tommy, recipients benefiting from the organ-donor program.

Years later, Judy told me that, one time while she was standing next to her son's hospital bed, with Tommy on life support, she cried out in anguish, "Why us? Why, Tommy?" All of a sudden, that inner voice we all have spoke to her very clearly. It asked, "Why not? Why not you and Tommy?" These words humbled her. Bad things happen to a lot of good people every day. Why should she and her family be any different? That is the message she got from her inner voice. She also came away with the distinct feeling that, in the dimension we all exist in before we are born, God told her she would give birth to a baby boy who would live to be only sixteen years old. It was just the way things were going to be, so enjoy and love him while you have him. No one lives forever on this earth. This belief in a predetermined plan has helped her tremendously to accept this tragedy in her life and move on as much as a mother can.

Judy sold her piano—she could no longer bring herself to play it. The joy that had inspired her to play the piano died with Tommy. She could not even bring herself to look at it. The piano represented a happier time, a time before a mother's incredible anguish from losing a child. Life does go on, but some things do not, cannot.

<hr>

Just as running put me in great health to survive my accident, over the months and years to come, running would help my sister survive the loss of her Tommy. She told me that she would run for miles and cry the whole time. Every time her running shoe hit the pavement, she was pounding out the anger and resentment that had built up in her mind and body—the anger of losing her son *and* the resentment that the other boys in the car had lived, with only minor scratches and bruises. She knew this feeling was wrong, but she could not help it. And, so, every day for the next fifteen years, she pounded her emotions into the pavement of the streets in her community, crying as she ran. Passing motorists would roll down their windows and ask her if she was alright, if she was hurt and needed a ride home. She did not answer;

she just looked straight ahead and ran and ran, tears streaming down her face. But she told me that running saved her. It was a distraction from her sorrow and provided a much-needed mental release. She also said that, had it not been for running and the support of her husband, she doubted that she would have survived the ordeal of losing Tommy.

<center>~~~~~~~~~~~~~~~~~~~~~~~~~~~~</center>

When Tommy died, I was almost forty. You'd think that, by then, I should have been a better person. I felt I should have been more enlightened and able to help soothe the brutal pain of losing a child. After all, I'd had the exceptional experience of dying and then coming back to life. I knew firsthand the divine nature of death, the unlimited power of love and faith. But I couldn't help my sister.

The problem was that I was an ordinary person who'd had an extraordinary encounter with God and heaven. In my mind, I should have been a better person because of it all. Why else had I survived? I should be helping other people in need. The knowledge I felt I possessed was not of this world. It was an acute understanding of life and, more importantly, death. I was unable to communicate that death was not only insignificant but that it's wonderful and beautiful.

This was the perfect opportunity, I thought, for God to use me for a higher purpose, to comfort people in need. I was right there, engulfed by grieving family and friends. The sorrow was palpable. *God, why aren't you using me to help others? Why did I survive against all odds, experience you firsthand, if not to help?* I was now more confused than ever. My sister wanted her son back. She did not want to hear that it was okay, that Tommy was in a beautiful place. He was dead, gone from her arms forever, and that is all that she could understand.

My *spirit* pulled me in one direction, letting me know I could do more to help than I was doing, but my *mind* told me not to—it told me I was a loser to whom no one would listen. This whole episode with Tommy pushed me over the edge. When this happened, I was only hanging on by a thread, mentally. And after sixteen years of what seemed like constant failure since my accident, Tommy's death finally broke me. I was overwhelmed with emotions from all directions: Tommy's death, my dismal job situation, the failure of my landscape company, my marriage on the rocks, no money to support my children—it was an avalanche of bad news that buried me, day after day. It wasn't just the loss of Tommy that was the final straw that broke my spirit—it was *me*.

I really feel that my experience of dying, existing in God's presence, and then coming back to life should make me better equipped to handle dire situations like this. Like most things in my new life, that thought was nothing but a hollow fantasy. All I could do was cry. I was a comfort to no one. I kept God's gift to me inside, when people I loved needed it the most. Chalk it up to another failure.

〜〜〜〜〜〜〜〜〜〜〜

I was down and out for the last time—this was it. I lacked the strength and the willingness to get up again. *I was done.* This "miracle recovery" I had gone through appeared to be nothing more than a long, drawn-out, painful death. Worst of all, it seemed like the only outstanding attribute of my new life was my ability to hurt people I cared about and to let them down. Why was God being so cruel? I died in my car accident. Why the "miraculous recovery"? I didn't ask for it. *I was content to be dead.*

I gave up. I gave up on everything. I just didn't care anymore. I lost my business, went into debt, and continued to drink, to numb it all. My attitude was "You can't squeeze blood from a stone." If I end up in jail, so be it. Maybe someone there would help me— no one else will.

After eleven years of marriage, Wendy and I got divorced. I can't blame her. I always struggled for money, and I still was not right in the head. I had my own large issues to deal with, so how could I be there for someone else when I didn't really know where I was coming from? It was doomed from the beginning. There was only one positive thing to come out of this union— actually, there are three of them: our beautiful and healthy children.

But when we got divorced, my heart was once again broken. Not by the loss of my wife, but by the loss of my three children. Even though I had them every weekend, the continuity of family was lost. I was devastated. All that I cared about and loved were my children. Over time, they would gravitate toward their mother, and I would feel more and more like an outsider looking in on my own family.

The first Christmas after the divorce was the worst. I woke up that morning in an empty house, without a family to celebrate the joy of Christmas.

I couldn't stand it, and I didn't want to start drinking so early, so I just put on my work clothes and went to work, even though it was Christmas Day. I had to stay busy, keep my mind occupied and try to block out the faces of my children I missed and loved so much. I worked for a large, nationwide tree company at the time, and had been working on a commercial account the previous week. There was simple and quiet work left to be done, and so I figured I could go do the work, stay busy, not charge for my time, and everyone would win.

Of course, people noticed I was working on Christmas Day, and they told my boss. The next day, he called me into his office, and I explained myself. He understood why I did it, but he requested that I let him know the next time I was going to do something like that, so he wouldn't be caught unawares.

~~~~~~~~~~~~~~~~~~~~~~~~~~~

Alone again and living by myself, I continued to make poor
~~~~~~~~~~~~~~~~~~~~~~~~~~~

choices, mostly having to do with girlfriends and alcohol. I had no self-esteem and was now my own worst enemy. It seemed impossible for me to break this loser cycle that my life had entered. I saw no way out. I felt I was too old and mentally deficient to go back to school to be retrained in a viable profession (plus I had no money), so I accepted my fate. I would live out what was left of my life doing menial, low-income work, if I could find it, and drink beer until everything went away. I started to build a wall around my life, my emotions. I didn't want to drag in anyone and pull them down to my level, ever again. It was self-defense. I had to protect what was left of me.

<center>~~~~~~~~~~~~~~~~~~~~~~~~~~</center>

Even with the additional income from shell fishing, I was in trouble and could not pay my bills. I will never forget the day I came back to my house after work—and the electricity had been shut off! This was just another low point in my life, and I thought to myself, *I survived a terrible car accident and an ensuing death experience for this? To be poor and struggle through life?* There has to be a better reason, a better life than this for me. It was not just my life that had to improve, either—I had three young children who deserved better than what I was giving them. I loved them dearly, but on that particular night, they were young, needed a warm meal, and most importantly to them, wanted to know when the TV was going to be fixed. How do you explain to your three little children you love so much that their father is a loser who has trouble keeping a job because of a car accident he was in before they were born?

I could not provide for my family, and I felt like such a failure as both a husband and father, so I resorted to taking the coward's way out of a situation: I drank a lot. I drank to gloss over the mess that was my life. More importantly, I wanted to forget that damn accident, forget my miraculous recovery, forget my death experience, forget God. But I could not forget any of it. I have tried to, but the physical scars on my forehead and the deformity of my skull remind me every time I look in the mirror. Every time I take my anti-seizure medication—three times a day—I remember. Every time something does not feel right in my body—a hand falls asleep, or there's numbness in my face, or I feel the simple spasm of a muscle, I fear it is the onset of another seizure, and I remember. Maybe God does not want me to forget.

I was running away from God when I should have been running to him. I should have remembered what my mother had told me as a child, "Turn your problems over to God." But God was not on my mind these hard days—survival was, and part of that misguided survival technique was to drink.

I brought my children back to their mother's house that night. I explained to Wendy that the power was out, and asked if the kids could stay with her, even though it was one of my days to have them. My ex-wife and I have always had a fairly good post-divorce relationship. Thankfully we both still lived in the same town, for the children's sake. Even so, divorce is a terrible thing to go through (so much for my neurologist's recommendation to avoid stress!). After returning to my cold house, with darkness slowly closing in and no electricity to turn on a light, I rejected the low-level life I thought I had no choice but to accept. I vowed to never be without money again. *Ever*.

Beg, borrow, and steal, if I had to—that was my new plan. Fortunately, the more practical solution was to do the crappy jobs that no one else wanted to do. I was scared by the risks I would take to earn a buck, but I would rather be dead than poor.

Divorced and living alone, my responsibilities were minimal. Either fortunately or unfortunately, there was a bar at the end of the street where I lived. Jake's Sports Tap. The draft beer was cheap and cold, and the eggs green. A real guy's bar. After working all day, I would lift weights at the gym and hit Jake's on the way home. I was working too hard, drinking too much, and I really didn't care. Alcohol was medicinal now. I needed to drink the pain away from my legs and back, and especially my forearms—they would go to sleep at night and be like wooden appendages that barely worked when I got up. No matter how many times this happened, my first thought was *Is this the onset of another seizure?* I would then have to talk myself through the process of understanding that I was alright, that no seizure was imminent. I worked, lifted, and drank beer. I was somewhat stable with my self-medication, but I knew I was drinking too much every night. I just didn't know how else to cope.

~ A Turning Point at Forty Feet Off the Ground ~

I had given up hope for any sort of normal life. I just did not seem to have what it took to earn a decent living, never mind be successful at anything. After many (about sixteen?) years of off-and-on work, I was desperate for a steady job. So, I responded to a help-wanted ad in the newspaper for a tree worker. Me, a tree worker? I knew nothing about tree work. I was hired because of the horticultural experience I'd gained in my failed attempt at running a landscape company. But more importantly, they were desperate for help.

Thankfully, the tree company that hired me was a large, nationwide outfit and was big into education and safety. I needed all the training and education I could get. I remember when I was a boy watching tree workers climb and prune the large elm trees on the village green in downtown Falmouth. As I watched, I thought to myself, *What kind of man did it take to climb sixty feet into the top of a tree, hang by a rope, and cut limbs with a chain saw?* As I was about to find out, *that kind of man* would eventually be me.

No matter how big and tough they think they are, a lot of guys do not make it in tree work, especially dragging brush. You don't have to worry about firing them; they just quit. Dragging brush is pulling cut limbs along the ground from where they fell to the wood chipper. Pile after pile, up and down stairs, through the woods, or along a street. It's one foot in front of the other as you drag as much weight as you can, drop it off at the chipper, and then head back for another pile.

Once you have put in your time dragging brush, the next progression up the ladder and pay scale is becoming a tree climber. When my boss thought I was ready, he taught me how to tie a climbing knot, the Blake hitch. Once I'd semi-mastered the knot, it was time for me to go up into a tree and see what I was made of.

As I drove to work one morning, I knew they were going to get me up into a tree that day. I was nervous and tried not to think about it. I arrived at the shop at my usual time, and the foreman of my crew was already there.

"Joey! How ya doin'? Today's a big day. Hope you stay out of the hospital." And he laughed, knowing that all rookie climbers are nervous—he called all rookies "Joey."

Aw, great, I thought. *That's a big vote of confidence.*

The day's job was all the way in Chatham, and the trip down

from the shop in Osterville seemed extra-long, as my nerves started to build. The job began as usual: Don ran the bucket truck, and I dragged brush and ran it through the chipper. Before lunch time arrived, Don decided it was time to get me up a tree, which was smart thinking—if you have an empty stomach, there is nothing to throw up.

"Okay, Joey. Let's get you up a tree," he said with a smile in his eye. He knew I was nervous, and seeing me squirm would be amusing.

"Uh, okay," I said tentatively. "What do I do?"

"Here, this is my climbing belt; put it on, but don't hurt nothing. I'll set your climbing line in the tree for you—you've got enough to worry about, ha-ha."

I nervously fumbled with the belt. You had to step through it, and not only did you have to cinch it tight around your waist like any belt, you also had to cinch two more smaller belts around each thigh. This made it almost impossible to slip out of the climbing belt, no matter what contortion your body may be going through.

"All right, Joey. Come over here! Hurry up! We don't have all day."

The belt was awkward to walk in, so I waddled over to the tree Donny had selected as a good "beginners" tree for me. I stood next to him at the base of the tree, looked up, and watched the top of the tree sway back and forth in the summer wind.

"You want me to climb that?" I asked incredulously. It was really a dumb question, seeing as how he had already set the climbing line about three quarters of the way up the forty-foot pine tree.

"Donny, look at the top going back and forth. Are you sure it's safe?" I squeaked.

"I've climbed hundreds of trees like this, and there's really no wind. You won't notice it once you're up there. Now, tie your climbing knot, and get up there!" he instructed.

I was scared and lacked self-confidence, but I at least had to try. I had tried and failed before in life. What difference would one more failure be on my ever-growing list?

The Blake hitch is just one variation of a friction hitch. Once a friction hitch slides up your rope, it will not come back down, unless you pull the knot down. This enables you to 1) climb a tree without slipping down your rope and 2) hang in a tree with both your hands free to work. I fumbled with the knot and tied it all wrong. I looked at Donny and said I needed some help.

"I'll help you now, Joey, but once you get as high as you can in the tree, you're going to have to untie your knot, put it through a different crotch, and tie your climbing knot all by yourself. So, you'd better pay attention."

"Yeah, yeah, okay. I'll remember," I said, but I knew I'd forget. I'd figure out a way to get down, or Donny would climb up and help me. That was my attitude. I expected I would fail and that somebody else would bail me out. It is something I should be ashamed of, but my pride had been destroyed years ago. I didn't care what other people thought of me now.

With my Blake hitch tied and line clipped into my climbing belt, I was all set to go.

"Alright, Joey. Stand on your tiptoes, and slide the climbing knot up the line as far as it will go," Don instructed.

I did as I was told.

With a smile, he asked, "How's that saddle feel? Ridin' up your ass? Ha, ha."

"What do I do now?" was all I could get out.

"Lean back on your rope, and put both of your feet on the tree."

"What?" This didn't seem right. "Are you joking with me?"

"All right—listen to me. This is serious time. You don't joke around with a rookie climber."

I could tell that he meant it.

"Now, lean back a little. You'll feel the rope starting to hold you up." I did as I was told, and, as I transferred some of my weight off my feet, it was picked up by the climbing line.

"Okay, Joey. Good. Now just pick up your feet, and put them on the tree, one foot at a time."

Left foot first, good job, now the right. It brought back painful memories of when I could barely walk across a room, never mind up a tree.

I put both of my feet on the tree and ...

"Whoa!"

I swung far to the right and immediately put both of my feet back on the ground.

"Donny, what happened?" I wanted to know.

"Look," he said, "sometimes when your feet leave the ground you're going to swing left or right. It's the way the rope is set in the tree. Now get up there. We have to get back to work."

I got my feet back on the tree, and, once I stopped swinging, I started to advance the Blake hitch up my climbing rope just like I'd been taught. There were no limbs for about the first ten feet up, so I had to rely on my climbing hitch to not let me fall. I wasn't far off the ground, but I had entered a whole new world. It's unnerving to not have your feet on the ground, to literally hang from a rope in a tree, with your body parallel to the ground. Thankfully, I finally reached some branches in the tree, but whatever comfort I found in having something to grip onto was quickly lost as I looked down and realized how far off the ground I was. Out of fear and nerves, I hung onto the branches all the more tightly now. I advanced my climbing knot as best I could, always with one arm hooked around the tree. I continued up the tree, going higher and higher, until I finally reached the crotch that the climbing line went through. The good news was that I had made it this far without killing myself. The bad news was that I had to untie the climbing knot, put it through another crotch a few feet higher, retie the knot, and get myself down. I turned around for some help from Donny, but he was lying down on his back in a comfortable bed of Boston ivy.

"Donny!" I yelled "What do I do now?"

"Joey, we talked about this. Hang on." He got up from his comfortable spot in the ivy and moved to where he could see me better.

"Okay. First thing—put your buck strap around the tree, and clip it into your climbing belt, like I showed you."

A buck strap is like a long belt (6-12 feet long and adjustable) that attaches from one side of your climbing belt to the other, at waist height. If you wrap this around the tree and snug it down, you can't fall or be "bucked" out of the tree.

"Like this?" I thought I'd clipped it into the right D ring.

"Yeah—that's good enough," he snickered.

"Now untie the Blake," Donny instructed.

I did as I was told. I had to release the tension in the climbing line first, which then puts all your weight on the buck strap, an unnerving shift in dynamics for a rookie climber. I was scared before; now, I was *petrified.*

"What now?" I asked, my voice getting higher. I couldn't look at Donny. I couldn't look down. Donny noticed this.

"Joey, look at me. C'mon, look down at me."

I was untied from the tree, standing on limbs, with both my arms wrapped tightly around the tree, supported by my buck strap.

"Joey, you have to trust me. Just look down at me."

I did trust and respect him, so I forced myself to look down.

"See that crotch to your left above your head?"

I hesitantly pointed to a crotch, as much as I could while literally hugging a tree.

"No, that's too small, the other one," he pointed. "Yes, that one. Now put the climbing line through it—that's right. Good. Clip it into the D ring that you took it off of, and tie your knot, using the tail, back onto the line that goes to the ground. You can do it, Joey. I know you can."

I wasn't so sure. The sway of the pine tree in the wind was very unnerving. I was sure it was going to break. I had to use both hands to tie the knot—there was no way of avoiding it. I had to let go of the tree and trust my buck strap and the branches my feet were on to not let me fall. I fumbled with the line and tied an unrecognizable knot that would not hold down a balloon.

"I can't do it!" I called out in desperation. "I can't tie the knot."

"You have to. Now relax, and I'll talk you through it. Take the tail—that's right. Wrap it around the line four times, and then put the end of the tail between the second and third wrap. Good—now tighten it up," he instructed.

I went to tighten the knot, and it unraveled into a limp mess.

"Donny, I can't do it!"

"What happened? You almost had it!"

I had given up in my life before. Instead of buckling down and fixing what seemed like an unfixable problem, it was easier to just give up. I was giving up now. I just wanted out of the tree. That's all I cared about.

"Donny, I can't do it. Just get me down," I said, accepting defeat.

"Joey, I can't get you down. You have to do it."

"But I can't. I'm scared."

"Everyone is scared their first time in a tree."

"I can't do it! You have to get me down."

"Listen to me." Donny's voice had changed, and I knew that his patience had worn out. "I can call the fire department to get you down, but then you're all done in the tree industry. No one will hire you. Is that what you want?"

This was it, then. I had reached another critical juncture in my life, at forty feet off the ground, in the top of a swaying pitch pine tree on a beautiful estate in Chatham. I can give up and take the easy way out, go home, drink, and continue the downward spiral of my life. Or I can apply myself and try to solve my problems instead of running away from them.

"Joey!" The lighthearted Donny was back. "Don't give up! You almost had it. Let's try it again."

Silence from me.

"Joey, you alright?"

"Yeah. I'm scared, but I'm okay," I finally answered. "I went to tighten the knot, and it just unraveled. I thought I had done everything else right."

"You have to pull the tail and the leading end of the rope at the same time, or it won't stay tight, Joey. Try that."

I did as told.

"That's better—not perfect, but better," I told him.

"Okay, get your climbing line taut. Undo your buck strap, and come on down. Take your time."

Easier said than done. I tightened the climbing line, undid the buck strap, and now I had to take my feet off the two branches that had served as secure perches and hang by a rope again. I kept one arm around the tree as long as I could, while the other hand slowly inched the Blake hitch down the climbing line. When my boots finally hit the ground, my knees were shaking, and my forearms were scratched and bloody. Donny was already back to work—he couldn't take any more time to baby-sit me. No one would be there to hold my hand next time I went up into a tree. The sooner I became self-reliant, the better.

I was taking off the climbing saddle when Donny came over to me.

"Joey, let me see that knot you tied." He picked it up and gave it a quick look. "You'd better practice your knot—what you tied we call 'the suicide knot'!" he said, snickering as he walked away.

I put away Donny's climbing saddle, coiled and stowed the climbing line. Put my hard hat back on, picked up my rake, and went back to work.

There was no fanfare when I finally got down out of the tree. It was expected of me. No one to tell me, "Hey, do you know what you just did?"

Because no one knew. But the truth was that I had just turned a huge corner in my life. I had chosen not to give up, but to stick with it and solve the problem confronting me, even though I was scared out of my mind and feared for my life. It was a small thing I did—hundreds of guys do it every day—but it was a life-changing moment for me. I didn't recognize the significance of it at the time, but the direction of my life had once again changed drastically, this time for the better. Because of a pine tree.

CHAPTER TEN

~ Tree Guy ~

~ Advanced Therapy ~

When I first started out in the tree industry, I wasn't being paid much, but what I got from this profession has been priceless. Tree work quickly became my advanced physical and mental therapy. The rigors of the work forced me to push my body to its limits, day after day, year after year. I froze in winter and sweated my ass off in summer. I dragged brush and climbed trees without stopping until I thought my heart would beat out of my chest. With my hearing protection on (because of the way it fits over my ear and rests on the top of my neck), I could hear the blood pounding through my carotid arteries, and it sounded like my head was going to explode.

At one of my yearly physicals, I told my doctor that I had chest pains, but that I was pretty sure it was just a strained muscle. He asked me if I wanted a stress test to make sure it wasn't my heart. I laughed out loud—at some point in my recovery, I had been put through a stress test (comparatively, it wasn't that stressful), and I told him, "In my line of work, every day is a stress test." He agreed, we didn't do one, and the pain was gone a few days later.

I just kept pushing ahead, daring a seizure to come back and get me, or for my body to let me down. If it was going to happen, I wanted to force it to happen now! I needed to know my physical limits. To this day, I have not found them.

As I gained confidence in my body's ability to function normally, actually above normal, my brain began to pick up the pace of its recovery as well. It was forced to. Being a competent and safe tree worker comes down to having your act together. The knowledge you need is vast, from knowing your knots and anticipating loads in rigging down a tree, to tree species and recognizing hidden hazards in a tree based on its health and root structure.

You either learned and learned fast, or someone got hurt—probably yourself. This pushed my mind to have to think, absorb, and retain knowledge. I was also forced to think through a job, and when things did not go according to plan, I had to adjust on the fly, often from the canopy of a tree. As part of our training we had to know and practice CPR and first aid, be familiar with electrical hazards, and practice aerial rescues. It was no joke, and when I became a foreman, the very real responsibility of taking care of my crew was something I did not take lightly. It forced me to be on my toes, to think clearly, and to always be ready for the unexpected. So much can go so wrong in a split second. Train, be prepared, think safety. Imagine a job going right; imagine the same job going wrong. What will you do? If the foreman—me—is down and out, who will lead the crew in a rescue? My guys gave me grief about my tedious preparations, but no one ever got seriously hurt working with me. Of course, things happened, but they were all minor. Several times I had to get stitches after cutting myself with a saw, learned the hard way that I was allergic to bee stings (once going into anaphylactic shock), suffered from heat stroke on more than one occasion, and had poison ivy so bad a couple of times that the pus that oozes out of the wounds soaked my work clothes, turned black and stiff, and stunk by the end of the day. I loved it all—it made me feel so alive! Most of all, I was thankful that my body could handle this abuse and not let me down with another seizure. If I could handle this, I knew that I could handle almost anything.

I had started the process of finding myself again, but this was not an overnight transformation. Twenty or so years after my accident, my mind was still healing. Some brain synapses were still slowly coming "back on line."

~~~~~~~~~~~~~~~~~~~~~~~~~~~~

Besides the very real possibility of having another seizure, the biggest fear I had was running out of money again. When I vowed to never be destitute ever again, I meant it, and I would die trying before I let that happen. Even though I was making a weekly paycheck working for someone else, I was also doing tree work on the weekends, for extra money, and on days when work was cancelled because of wind, rain, snow, or ice. When weather conditions were deemed too dangerous for tree climbing, I would do my own tree jobs. I didn't care; I took a lot of risks. I'd show up on the jobsite in my mini-van packed full of climbing gear, kids car seats, ropes, and chainsaws. My transportation may not have been professional, but my work was.

Word spread fast throughout the community that I did great work and was reasonably priced. Before long, I had enough of a customer base that I decided to go out on my own and start my own tree company. I am good at sales, and people tend to like me, so my small company grew as I bought trucks and chippers,
~~~~~~~~~~~~~~~~~~~~~~~~~~~~

and hired employees.

I had come a long way from being on life support.

~~~~~~~~~~~~~~~~~~~~~~~~~~~~

As good as tree work has been, it has also taken its toll on my body. Years of tightly gripping a climbing line, using a twelve-foot-pole saw in the canopy of a tree, the wear and tear that climbing spikes put on knees, the pain a climbing saddle can inflict on hips, groin, private parts, it all adds up. Starting a chainsaw thousands of times, the vibration from operating a chainsaw both in the tree and a bigger one on the ground, dragging brush, lifting logs, raking debris both right and left handed, hefting a full debris bucket onto a shoulder, and then dumping it into the back of a chip truck—these are only a handful of the elements that make up a very tough job.

At night, my forearms ached, my hands were numb, and my back hurt. Just getting out of bed in the morning and putting on my socks was a painful challenge. At the height of my climbing days, I drank a lot. I was literally drinking the pain away so I could sleep at night. It also helped me not to focus on the numbness in various parts of my body and what it might
~~~~~~~~~~~~~~~~~~~~~~~~~~~~

mean—I could not be bothered by having another seizure. I was up and running in my new life, and nothing was going to stand in my way.

~ **Robbie** ~

Whatever happened to Robbie, my friend who was in the crash with me? I think we saw each other once after the accident, while we were both recovering. I don't think the visit went well. I got the feeling that Robbie blamed me for the crash and his resulting injuries. Then again, I was a shell of my former self. He may have been uncomfortable around me—the friend he had once known was long gone. I would have been weak and frail, slurring my words, with the big scars on my head still very prominent. His parents have moved out of town, to where I do not know. Through mutual friends, I have heard that Robbie is married and working in management for a large restaurant chain.

That is all that I know regarding my friend, Robbie, with whom I died.

~ You've Recovered Well, Tree Guy ~

I've had friends for years who knew nothing about my accident and related injuries. When I first decided to write my book, I was anxious for feedback from a new close friend whose opinion I highly respected. I told him a quick synopsis of my story, expecting anything but what he said. He simply replied, "You've recovered well," and I knew that conversation was over.

I was dumbstruck. I didn't know how to respond. He was right. I had recovered well, and that should make my story even more compelling. But instead, it seemed to give him permission to dismiss my struggle to become the normally functioning person and friend he had come to know. All of my new friends saw only the strong and healthy "tree guy" who ran his own, successful company.

I was speaking to another friend, Julie, about my experience and could see the disbelief on her face as I talked about "pulverized, liquefied brain matter," so I pointed to the scar on my forehead and asked her, "Did you ever notice this scar?"

"Oh, yes," she replied without hesitation.

"How do you think I got it?" I asked.

Today, the only visible scar I have is the one Dr. Weaver made during emergency brain surgery—he used the same place to go back in and install my plate. (The original scar from the accident itself is more of a jagged tear across my head and has long since faded.) I remember Dr. Weaver proudly showing me how he had purposely led the incision into the furrows of skin that naturally occurred when my forehead wrinkled, so the scar would not be so noticeable. It was a nice try, but the scar is too long. This scar is also nice and straight, obviously the work of a skilled surgeon, and it has not faded, having been opened up twice.

Julie answered, "I just assumed you got it doing tree work."

"The Tree Guy." That is how my new friends know me, and my old friends see me that way as well. Not that I want to dwell on it, but it makes my thirty-six-year recovery and struggle to be somewhat normal again, which is so meaningful and important to me, a non-factor to everyone else.

This lack of interest further illustrates just how alone I have been in my recovery. The only person who asks how I am doing in regard to my accident is my neurologist, and that's his job. It has been decades since anyone else has asked me how I am doing relating to the injuries I suffered. No one has ever questioned me about my death experience, which I find odd but understandable.

I still see a neurologist once a year, and I continue to pass all his tests. Sometimes we talk about things in general, but I know he is listening for abnormalities in my speech and thought process, and that is fine. I am not worried about it. What does bother me is the condition of the other patients waiting to be seen. They are of all ages and look like they really need help. I am reminded of how lucky I really am. I never take the elevator up to the floor where his office is. I always take the stairs running—I refuse to go up any flight of stairs one step at a time, as it brings back bitter memories of my struggle to walk again. Memories I choose to leave very far behind me.

I am fit, clean shaven, and looking the best that I can—I have ceased to notice or care about the scar on my head. I know that people look at me and wonder why I'm there at the neurologist. *He must be a hypochondriac*, they're probably thinking. I appear so healthy. If only they knew the long and hard road I've followed over the last thirty-six years. On the rare occasion when someone does ask why I'm there—and they have—I say I was in a bad car accident when I was twenty-three years old. That usually ends the conversation. It's all they care to know and all I care to say about it.

I still occasionally say and do stupid things. I know when this happens that it is due to the part of my brain that is still not right. I sometimes have trouble thinking—not as much as I used to, but it still happens. Recently, a ringing in my ears developed, particularly my right one. I was run through a CAT Scan unit, looking for abnormalities in my head. The only comment from the doctor who read the CAT Scan is that I was missing part of my brain, just beneath the plate in my skull. Tough news to hear about yourself, but it really doesn't matter now.

I am thankful for my second chance at this life, but also still confused by it. Do I simply accept it on face value and not probe for a deeper meaning? What about my medically unexplainable overnight recovery? What about the faith healing and prayers that I could feel washing over and healing my body? My angel from the ICU, my crazy dreams of dying, being dead, and coming back to life? I cannot simply ignore all of this. I have tried. It won't let me.

When I first decided to write about what happened to me, I went to see an old friend, Cindy, who I knew would be receptive to what I was writing about. I had written only eleven pages, and they were mostly about my death experience. I was so excited to share the incredible things that happened to me. She took my "manuscript," and we agreed to talk in a few days. I half-expected her to call me up, breathlessly exclaiming, "Jimmy, I read your story. Did this really happen to you? Oh, my God!"

But she did not call. After three days, I called her, still sort of anticipating the same reaction.

"Hi, Cindy. It's Jim. Did you get a chance to read my story?" I asked anxiously.

"Yes, yes I did. It's really nothing more than an essay."

"What? I'm sorry—what did you say?"

"It's not very long; it's just an essay," she repeated.

An essay! No, it's life and death, dying and being in heaven with God, and then coming back to life again. That's what happened to me, and I'm on the other end of the phone with you—don't you want to know more?

That's what I thought, not what I said.

My actual reply was, "Oh, I'm sorry. I didn't mean to waste your time."

"That's okay. Keep working on it—you may have something here. Call me if I can help."

"Okay. Thanks, I'll be in touch." *No, I won't*, I thought. It took a lot for me to write about a small part of what I had been through. I was all done with writing. I never should have tried.

Before I could hang up, though, I heard Cindy's voice, "Jimmy … Jimmy, are you still there?"

"Yes, I'm here."

"Jimmy, I don't know if you're aware of it or not, but Ray passed away a few months ago."

I was caught off guard. I had heard that her husband Ray committed suicide.

"Yes, I am aware of that, and I am so sorry for your loss. Ray was a great guy."

My tree company did work for Ray and Cindy at least once a

year, and he was indeed a great guy. His death made no sense to me, especially suicide.

"Jimmy, can I ask you something?"

"Of course, Cindy. Anything."

"Please don't think I'm weird, but I need to know something."

"Okay."

"Jimmy, Ray killed himself. I found him in his Jaguar in the garage."

"I'd heard something like that. It must have been so hard for you. I'm so sorry."

"Jimmy, is he all right? I love him so much, and I can't sleep at night worrying about him." An odd concept. Is someone who is dead okay? Cindy knew it, but she couldn't bear the thought of her beloved husband in pain, suffering.

Without hesitating, I answered, "Cindy, there are some things I just know from when I was dead. I don't know how I know them—I just do. One of the things I know is that when we die, *we are all more than okay*. More importantly, no one is excluded from the beauty of heaven. It is beautiful beyond our comprehension, and we exist in the warmth and light of love."

A pause on the other end of the phone, a sniffle prompted by tears. "But the church says that if you kill yourself … sniffle … you don't go to heaven. He was too good of a man not to go to heaven, Jimmy—you know that!" The thought of the man she loved for all the years of their marriage being denied a place in heaven caused anger to surge through her tears.

"It doesn't matter," I told her. "I know this beyond a shadow of a doubt. It is one of the strongest feelings I came away with. Ray is with God. He is at peace, wrapped in love. He is home."

Through the sobs, she said, "Oh, thank you, Jimmy. Thank you."

After we hung up, the thought occurred to me: Maybe that is why I survived my crash and all the following difficult years. I was spared for that one conversation, five minutes of consoling a grieving widow about the well-being of her dead husband.

I have accepted that possibility, and I am good with it.

CHAPTER ELEVEN

~ A Power That Defies Description ~

$\mathscr{T}$he janitor of the congregational church slowly closed the two large wooden doors that make up the front entrance. *Another week, another good service*, he thought. He then turned his attention to straightening up the pews, putting the hymnals back in their brackets, and picking up any papers left behind. With that task complete, he headed up to the altar and pulpits. This area was always left clean, but he checked it anyway.

"Huh," he said in surprise as he scanned the top of the pulpit. *Nathan left the prayer list up here today. Good thing I checked,* he thought and picked up the handwritten list.

On a table in the narthex lay a pen and pad of paper, provided for parishioners to write down the names of people who are sick or in need of help. No specifics are given as to why the name was on the list—that is irrelevant. This was the prayer list for the morning service. It was simple and hand-written on a cheap pad of manila paper—nothing fancy, hardly worthy of God's attention. At the same point in the service every week, Nathan, the minister, read off the names as everyone prayed for that person or at least that name:

Jessica …

David …

Suzanne …

… and the list goes on.

"Amen," the congregation said in unison. The prayer was over; the service continued, as if trying to communicate with God had never happened. There was no crack of lightning or mighty crash of thunder to announce that a miraculous answer to a long-shot prayer was being answered.

The janitor picked up the list and quickly glance's at the names. They'd all been written using the same pen, but the handwriting was different for each one.

Why bother? he wondered. *Is this a "Hail, Mary"*—he smiled at the religious humor—*for a lost cause? When all else has failed, turn to God and prayer?*

He crumpled up the paper and shoved it in his pocket, to be thrown into the trash when he got downstairs.

A pen, some paper, and prayer? This is all we have to battle cancer? To console a grieving family over the loss of a child? Or help a broken young man on life support whose brain has been partially pulverized in a car accident? It seems pathetically little, more designed to give a feeling of contributing to the grieving when they are otherwise helpless in an overwhelmingly bad situation. *But this is faith at its finest.* The chips are down, if not gone, and there is nothing that you can do but pray. Money, influence, power, and intelligence are all rendered useless by the susceptibility of our bodies and minds to devastating situations that are completely out of our control.

Hardly, if ever, do we get to see the positive end result of what or who we pray for, and we never will. *We do it anyway.*

~ Faith in Action~

As I lay comatose in the ICU, more dead than alive, my name was added to the prayer list of at least two churches in town that I know of, probably more. Dr. Weaver told my parents, "Medically, we have done all that we can do—now it is up to Jim and God."

The faith healers, Joy and Kay, told my sister Marty, "Jim is now trying to decide between living and dying."

I recall this happening to me:

I was lying on my back on a nondescript bed. The white sheets that covered me from the waist down were glowing with a white light. The walls were covered by a soft linen, and they were glowing with white light as well. There was a very intense light that hovered inches above my chest and was only as wide as my body. This blindingly bright light moved slowly over me, warming me to my core and healing my body as it passed over it.

This is the faith and love that are contained in prayer at work.

This is when the intense light of prayer penetrated deep into my body, into the microscopic cells that made up me. This is where my healing began in the minuscule places that no scalpel or suture could ever reach. It is not limited to the physical—the healing light of prayer also reached into my mind, changing my attitude.

This is what happened to me. I remember experiencing this wonderful feeling of being engulfed in love and healed by the faith and love contained in prayer.

That is the power of prayer—beautiful in its simplicity, mysterious in its results, defeating disease and death, soothing hurt and pain. It is an action that starts in the brain, tempered by a belief in something bigger than ourselves—God, if you will— and comes from the heart.

It is easy. It is pure, and the results can be phenomenal.

Prayer, at least in my case, was not an absolute—its power brought me back from death and gave me a fighting chance. It brought me up from the depths of my injuries to a point where I could survive. During this critical time over the weeks following my crash, that may be all people prayed for—"Please don't let Jim die. Bring him back to us." And that is what happened. I am living proof that prayer works, that miracles do happen.

There is a "home" made of love waiting for all of us when we die. Our arrival there is anticipated. It is *our* place, where we belong for eternity. Knowing this to be true, I can live, and die, without fear.

***

APPENDIX A:

Cape Cod Hospital Clinical Resume

CAPE COD HOSPITAL

27 Park Street/Hyannis, MA 02601/(617) 771-1800

JAMES HOLMES
#22-65-32

CLINICAL RESUME

ADMISSION: /2-17-80
DISCHARGE: 1-13-81

This 23-year-old man involved in an automobile accident, brought to the emergency room of Cape COd Hospital for neurosurgical evaluation. He seemed to be comatose at the accident site and having some respiratory distress.

PAST MEDICAL HISTORY: Not immediately available. In retrospect, family states that he has been in excellent general health with no medical problems that would have a bearing on the present illness.

PHYSICAL EXAMINATION: On admission, the patient had signs of serious cranial trauma, with multiple scalp lacerations, contusions, and subgaleal hematomas. There was also evidence of probable facial and periorbital fractures. Respiratory embarrassment was present and corrected by endotracheal intubation. Blood pressure was mildly elevated. Pulse slow with frequent premature ventricular contractions. General survery revealed probable multiple rib fractures on the right, anterior and posterior right acromioclavicular separation, numerous contusions and minor abrasions of the body and legs with no gross fracture deformities. ABDOMEN: soft, no palpable masses. PELVIC: seems stable.

HOSPITAL COURSE: The patient was seen to have a serious head injury. Computer scan demonstrated multiple intercerebral hematomas from contusion, a modest subdural hematoma and considerable edema of the white matter. Craniotomy was accomplished and a laceration of brain with active bleeding, controlled by debridement and usual hemastatic measures. Several smaller intercerebral hematomas were evacuated along with the subdural hematoma. The patient was placed in Intensive Care Unit with careful monitoring of blood gas studies and attempts made to keep intercranial pressures low via the usual measures of osmotic diuretics, steroids, and controlled hyperventilation. A pneumothorax developed that required placement of a chest tube on the right side and this expanded and the tube could finally be removed with minimal residual air collection, gradually resolving. Facial fractures were noted and felt to be of no clinical significance at this time, to be evaluated at a later date by the plastic and oral surgeons. The patient made remarkable progress and was extubated. He began to move symmetrically and eventually started incoherent verbalization. This also improved to reasonably coherent communication, and finally satisfactory general orientation. (

YOUR NON-PROFIT COMMUNITY HOSPITAL

HOLMES, JAMES   -   SUMMARY   -   CONTINUED   -   PAGE TWO

Bilateral extensor toe responses cleared and the strength of his left side improved to only a mild to moderate hemiparesis. He was transferred from the Intensive Care Unit and vigorous physical therapy instituted. Follow-up computer scan showed clearing of the edema and relatively normal ventricular contour. Finally, he was discharged to home care, hesitantly ambulatory, with fair strength on his left side. Follow-up care planned with the neurosurgeons and with the general surgical, plastic and oral surgeon consultants, along with orthopedic evaluation of his acromioclavicular separation.

FINAL DIAGNOSIS: 1. Head injury, (with multiple intracranial hematomas).
                    Subdural hematoma.
                    Laceration of brain, right hemisphere.
2.   Multiple facial fractures.
3.   Pneumothorax, right.
4.   Multiple rib fractures, right.
5.   Acromioclavicular separation, right.

PROCEDURE: Craniotomy for evacuation of subdural hematoma; repair of lacerated brain; evacuation of multiple intercranial hematomas; insertion of chest tube, right, for correction of pneumothorax times two.

APPENDIX B:

Cape Cod Hospital Operative Record

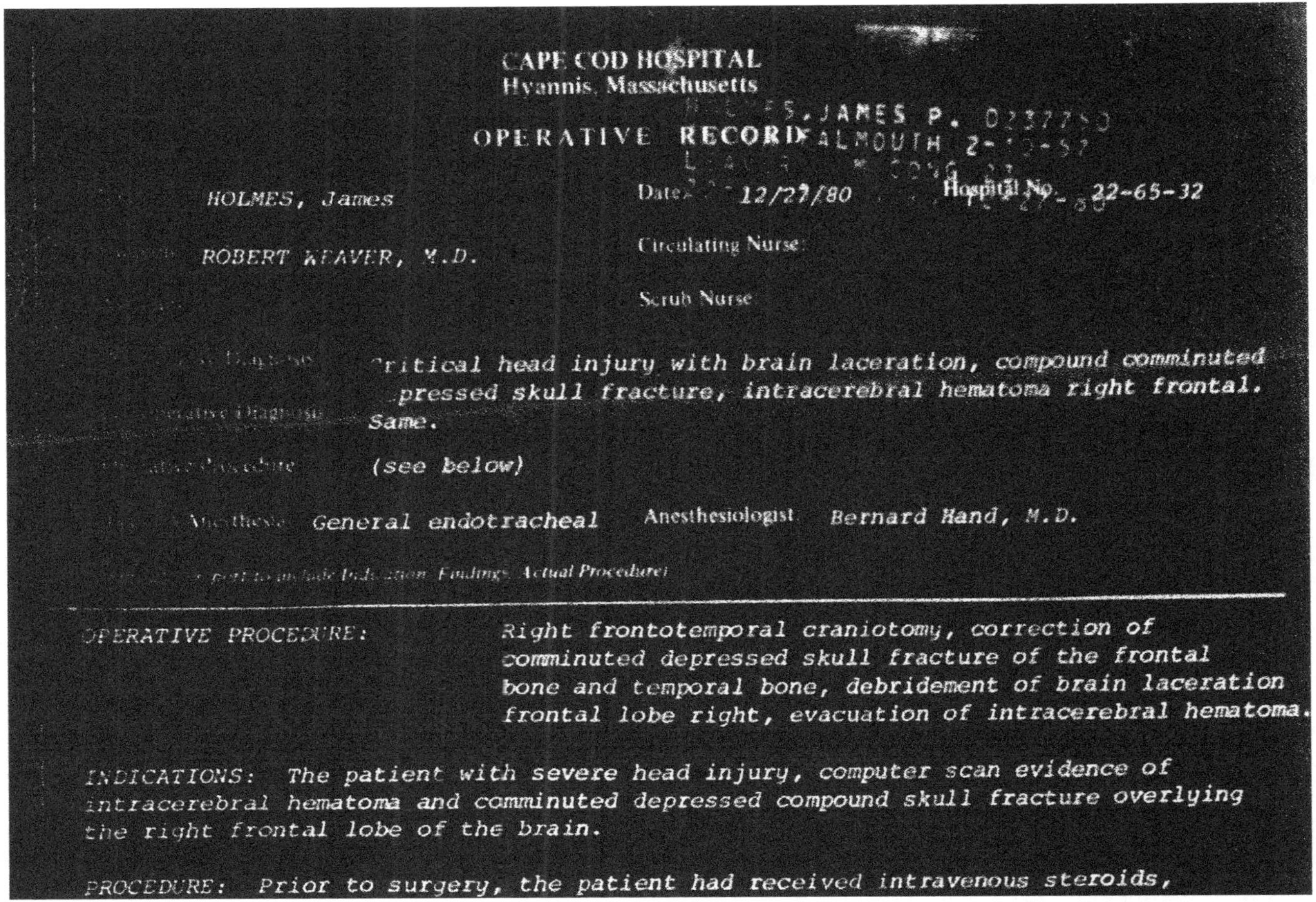

CAPE COD HOSPITAL
Hyannis, Massachusetts

...S, JAMES P.
OPERATIVE RECORD FALMOUTH

HOLMES, James — Date 12/27/80 — Hospital No. 22-65-32

ROBERT WEAVER, M.D. — Circulating Nurse:

Scrub Nurse

Critical head injury with brain laceration, compound comminuted depressed skull fracture, intracerebral hematoma right frontal.

Same.

(see below)

General endotracheal — Anesthesiologist Bernard Hand, M.D.

(Report to include Indication, Findings, Actual Procedure)

OPERATIVE PROCEDURE: Right frontotemporal craniotomy, correction of comminuted depressed skull fracture of the frontal bone and temporal bone, debridement of brain laceration frontal lobe right, evacuation of intracerebral hematoma.

INDICATIONS: The patient with severe head injury, computer scan evidence of intracerebral hematoma and comminuted depressed compound skull fracture overlying the right frontal lobe of the brain.

PROCEDURE: Prior to surgery, the patient had received intravenous steroids, intracerebral hematoma and comminuted depressed compound skull fracture overlying the right frontal lobe of the brain.

PROCEDURE: Prior to surgery, the patient had received intravenous steroids, diuretics and antibiotics. The entire head was prepared and sterily draped. A frontotemporal scalp flap was then outlined utilizing a sizable frontal laceration as its base. Several holes were placed in the frontal and temporal bone with the gas powered drill and these were connected with the craniotome. Several large segments of bone that were comminuted and depressed were then elevated along with the major bone flap. As this was done, pulverized liquified brain material came forth in the epidural space from a rent in the dura about 3 cm. in length, probably over the superior frontal gyrus at about its mid point. The dura was opened widely and reflected. The laceration was inspected after hemostasis was obtained with the bipolar forceps. Numerous intracerebral hematomas and devitalized white matter was noted. No single large cavity of hematoma was present, rather numerous grape sized collections of black blood. These were evacuated through the small cortical incision. The brain then seemed to relax a bit and began to undulate normally. Avitene was placed in the dissection bed and no attempt was made to close the dura. A large piece of Gelfoam was placed over the cortex and moistened. The temporalis muscle was placed over the dural opening and sutured into place. A Jackson-Pratt drain was placed from the subdural space under the muscle and out through a separate stab wound. Because of the nature of the problem and the compound wound to the bone, it was felt prudent to not replace the skull pieces. The scalp was closed with neurolon suture, a dressing applied. The sponge and cottonoid count correct. Estimated total blood loss was less than 400 c.c., not requiring acute replacement. The patient returned to the ICU in critical but somewhat improved condition.

:   12/27/80
:   1/6/81/kt   ROBERT WEAVER, M.D.

"Only when we are no longer afraid, do we begin to live."

Dorothy Thompson.

Please visit my you-tube channel (Jim Holmes Pen, Paper, Prayer) Where I will be posting a series of weekly videos as a companion to my book. As I like to call it, these videos will be the, "story within the story" as told by me.

I am doing this so, you, the reader can go on this journey with me. It is important that you get involved, ask me questions, and together we will try to understand the mystery of death.

Simultaneously we can explore the miracles that allowed me to survive not only a severe brain injury but the actual loss off part of my brain. We will laugh, cry and hopefully come away with a greater appreciation of this life while learning not to fear the next.

Don't forget to "Like" and "Subscribe"

Visit my website at https://jamespholmes.com